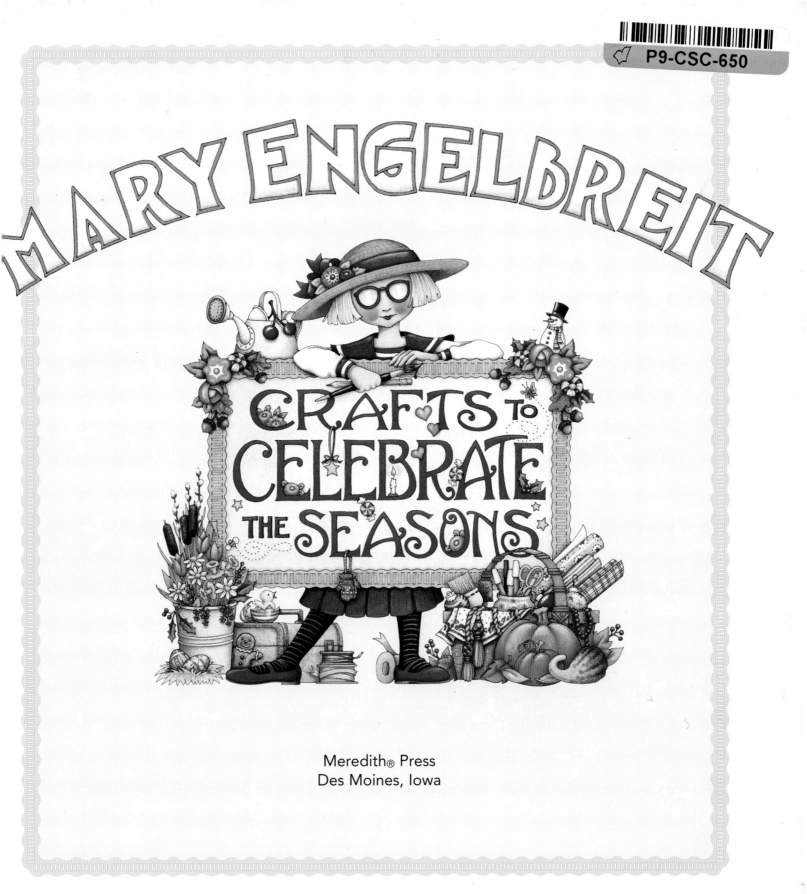

MARY ENGELBREIT

CRAFTS TO CELEBRATE THE SEASONS

Meredith® Press
Des Moines, Iowa

Meredith® Press
An imprint of Meredith® Books

Mary Engelbreit: Crafts to Celebrate the Seasons
Editor: Carol Field Dahlstrom
Technical Editor: Susan M. Banker
Graphic Designer: Angie Haupert Hoogensen
Copy Chief: Catherine Hamrick
Copy and Production Editor: Terri Fredrickson
Contributing Copy Editor: Diane Doro
Contributing Proofreaders: Colleen Johnson,
    Sheila Mauck, JoEllyn Witke
Technical Illustrator: Chris Neubauer Graphics, Inc.
Electronic Production Coordinator: Paula Forest
Editorial and Design Assistants: Judy Bailey,
    Mary Lee Gavin, Karen Schirm
Production Director: Douglas M. Johnston
Production Manager: Pam Kvitne
Assistant Prepress Manager: Marjorie J. Schenkelberg
Photographers: Peter Krumhardt, Andy Lyons
    Cameraworks, Scott Little
Project Designers: Susan M. Banker, Carol Dahlstrom,
    Phyllis Dunstan, Margaret Sindelar, Alice Wetzel

Meredith® Books
Editor in Chief: James D. Blume
Design Director: Matt Strelecki
Managing Editor: Gregory H. Kayko

Director, Sales & Marketing, Retail:
    Michael A. Peterson
Director, Sales & Marketing, Special Markets:
    Rita McMullen
Director, Sales & Marketing, Home & Garden Center
    Channel: Ray Wolf
Director, Operations: George A. Susral

Vice President, General Manager: Jamie L. Martin

Meredith Publishing Group
President, Publishing Group: Christopher M. Little
Vice President, Consumer Marketing & Development:
    Hal Oringer

Meredith Corporation
Chairman and Chief Executive Officer: William T. Kerr

Chairman of the Executive Committee: E. T. Meredith III

Cover Illustration: Mary Engelbreit Studios

All of us at Meredith® Press are dedicated to providing you with information and ideas to create beautiful and useful projects. We welcome your comments and suggestions. Write to us at: Meredith® Press, Crafts Editorial Department, 1716 Locust St., Des Moines, IA 50309-3023.

If you would like to purchase copies of any of our books, check wherever quality books are sold.

 is a registered trademark of Mary Engelbreit Enterprises, Inc.

seasons to celebrate!

From the time I was a little girl, I have always loved the seasons. Growing up in the heart of the Midwest, I had the pleasure of experiencing the seasons transition from winter wonderlands to sun-soaked days. I can recall jumping in the leaves with my dog, Ivy, and building snowmen families with my sisters, Alexa and Peggy.

I do love the elements the seasons enrich us with—colorful leaves during fall, bright blossoms during spring and summer, and pinecones during winter. These are the gifts of the seasons—all of which can be incorporated in crafting themes throughout your home and lifestyle.

Whether it's decorating spring eggs, creating vases for your summer bouquet, carving fall pumpkins, or stitching fleece mittens—you'll discover wonderful craft ideas to celebrate and welcome every season!

Enjoy!

Mary Engelbreit

contents

CHAPTER 1autumn

The vibrant colors and symbols of the season come alive in this inspiring chapter brimming with fun-to-do crafts to show your love of autumn.

CHAPTER 2winter

Create a merry season for those dear to your heart with trims and treasures you can make.

CHAPTER 3 spring

As flower buds awaken and gently make their way into the world, renew your sense of creativity by crafting springtime sensations as fresh as the season itself.

CHAPTER 4 summer

Bring the beauty of summer inside with clever things to make for the table— including a collection of vases to fill with blooms from the garden.

autumn

The colors are breathtaking...there's a chill in the air...
it's time to celebrate AUTUMN! Come craft your way
into this refreshing time of year with welcoming wreaths to
make, personality-plus pumpkins to carve, and floor mats
to paint with all the colors of the season! Turn the page to
discover a bounty of ideas inspired by autumn.

mantel pumpkin patch

Expressions of all kinds light up this gathering of pumpkins made from bell cups perched on bent-wire stems.

WHAT YOU'LL NEED

Purchased striped or solid bell cups on wrapped wires (available in the dried floral section of crafts and discount stores)

Acrylic paints in black, orange, and yellow

Paintbrushes

Tracing paper

Pencil

Scissors

Small terra-cotta pots

Permanent black marker

Styrofoam blocks

Wire cutter, optional

Popcorn and candy corn

HERE'S HOW

1. Paint some of the bell cup tops with orange paint. Leave some of the striped bell cups unpainted.

2. Trace the patterns, *pages 10–11*, onto tracing paper and cut out. Trace around the patterns on the terra-cotta pots and the painted bell cups.

3. Paint the faces on the pots and the bell cups using yellow paint. Let the paint dry. Outline the painted shapes with black marker.

4. Paint the rims of the terra-cotta pots as desired, adding stripes, dots, or other motifs. Let the paint dry.

5. Cut large pieces of Styrofoam to fill the pots, leaving about 1 inch at the top. If desired, bend the stems of the bell cups before sticking them into the Styrofoam. To make a spiral, wrap the stem around a dowel. To make a zigzag, bend the stem back and forth about every inch. Decide how to arrange the pumpkins and trim the stems, if necessary, to reach the desired height. Stick the bell cup stems into the Styrofoam.

6. Fill the pots and bell cups with popcorn and candy corn.

mantel pumpkin patch —
terra-cotta pot patterns

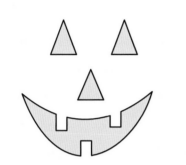

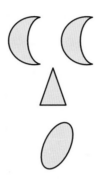

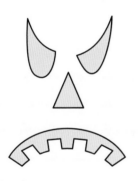

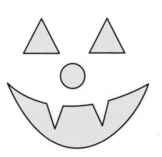

mantel pumpkin patch —
pumpkin face patterns

trick-or-treat floor mat

A clever painting technique creates the illusion of a bed of leaves that frames the bold message on this colorful Halloween floor mat.

WHAT YOU'LL NEED

18x24-inch piece of vinyl flooring
Gesso
Ruler
Masking tape
Paper
Model spray paints in sunflower
  yellow, orange, and transparent
  metallic green
Leaves
Acrylic paints in white, black, blue,
  purple, yellow, orange, and green
Foam plate
Natural sponge
Flat paintbrush
Alphabet sponges
Pencil with round-tip eraser
Black permanent marker
Gloss polyurethane

(continued on pages 14–15)

HERE'S HOW

1. Paint the back side of the vinyl with gesso. Allow to dry.

2. Measure 5 inches in from all edges and draw a border. Leaving the 5-inch border area exposed, place masking tape along the inside edges of the marked rectangle. Cover the rectangle with paper, taping it in place.

◀ **4.** Spray random light spots of orange over the yellow, being careful not to spray too much.

▼ **5.** Position leaves randomly in the border area. When the leaves are placed as desired, spray over the entire border area with green, lightly covering the surface. When dry, remove the leaves to reveal the pattern.

▲ **3.** Spray a base coat of yellow on the 5-inch border area.

▼ 8. Arrange the sponge letters onto the surface of the mat spelling the words "TRICK OR TREAT." Place yellow paint onto a plate, spread it out, and dip the first sponge evenly into the paint. Carefully stamp onto the surface. Repeat the process until the words are completed.

▲ 6. Adhere masking tape to leave a ¾-inch border. Paint the border white. When dry, paint in black checks using a ¾-inch flat brush and single strokes. Let the paint dry.

▶ 7. Remove the tape and paper from the center of the mat. Tape off the border. Put blue and purple paints onto a foam plate. Dip the sponge into the paint and dab on the center of the mat. Continue sponging the center until the entire area is covered and blended to the desired stage. Let the paint dry.

9. Add different colored dots onto the background using the eraser end of a pencil dipped into paint and dotted onto the surface. Let the paint dry.

10. Outline the checkered border and the letters with a black permanent marker. Coat the surface with two coats of gloss polyurethane. Let the polyurethane dry. Store the mat flat. Folding or rolling the mat may cause cracking.

pumpkins in a row

gold-leafed pumpkin

jester pumpkins, *below*, and beribboned pumpkin, *opposite*

decorated
pumpkins

Lining the walkway or arranged on the table,

these fun pumpkins will add merriment when

little ghouls and goblins come to call.

Instructions for all pumpkins start on page 19.

polka-dot pumpkins

pumpkins in a row

See photograph, page 16.

WHAT YOU'LL NEED

Four pumpkins
Carving knife
Spoon
Weathered board
Nails with large flat heads
Hammer

HERE'S HOW

1. Cut the pumpkins in half vertically just beyond the stem. Use the pumpkin halves that have the stems attached. Scoop out the insides.
2. Carve desired faces in each of the pumpkin halves.
3. Arrange the carved pumpkins on a board and nail in place.

gold–leafed pumpkin

See photograph, page 16.

WHAT YOU'LL NEED

Pumpkin
Leaves that are pliable and not too dry or brittle
Glue stick
Gold spray paint

HERE'S HOW

1. Use nicely shaped leaves that are pliable and not cracking. Place small dabs of glue on the backs of the leaves. Use just enough to hold the leaves on momentarily, so that they can be removed. Position leaves onto the pumpkin beginning at the top working downward. Stop about halfway down.
2. After all leaves are positioned as you like, begin to spray the pumpkin with gold paint. Cover the top well, working downward and fading the spray off about halfway down. The bottom half will have no paint. Carefully remove the leaves from the pumpkin, leaving a pattern. Let the paint dry.
3. To create a bed of leaves for the pumpkin, spraypaint extra leaves gold on both sides. Let the paint dry. Arrange the leaves beneath the pumpkin.

beribboned pumpkin

See photograph, page 17.

WHAT YOU'LL NEED

Pumpkin
Spool of 1-inch-wide purple ribbon
¼-inch-wide metallic gold ribbon
Gold upholstery tacks
Scissors

HERE'S HOW

1. With a spool of purple ribbon, begin at the top of the pumpkin and pin the ribbon in place, using a gold upholstery tack.
2. Bring the ribbon down under the center, tack at the bottom, and bring back around to the top. Repeat this process two or three more times.
3. After all of the ribbons are attached, add extra tacks for decoration, spacing them evenly on the ribbon. Tie a ribbon bow around the stem using both the purple and gold ribbons.

polka–dot pumpkins

See photograph, opposite.

WHAT YOU'LL NEED

Pumpkin
Acrylic paints in black and white
Paintbrush
Pencil with round-tip eraser
Green raffia and artificial cherries, optional

HERE'S HOW

1. Wash and dry the pumpkin.
2. Paint the entire pumpkin, including the stem, with either black or white paint. Let dry.
3. Dip the eraser end of a pencil into the contrasting color of paint and dot the surface of the pumpkin. Continue making dots on surface as many times as desired. Let dry.
4. Use the contrasting paint to create a checkerboard pattern on the stem of the pumpkin. Let dry.
5. Tie a raffia bow around the stem of the pumpkin. Tuck cherry stems into raffia.

jester pumpkins

See photograph, page 16.

WHAT YOU'LL NEED

Tracing paper
Pencil
Scissors
Pumpkins
Felt in favorite colors
Fine gold wire
Gold upholstery tacks

HERE'S HOW

1. Trace the patterns, *right* and *opposite*, onto tracing paper and cut out. Cut star shapes from felt.

▼ **2.** Cut two slits in the center of the stars just large enough to fit the stem through. Place the larger star over the stem. Pull the points firmly down and hold in place with upholstery tacks.

▶ **3.** Add a smaller star of a different color over the top of the first one, tacking down the points.

4. Curl fine gold wire around the stem. Cut several extra large stars to place underneath the pumpkin, if desired.

**jester pumpkin —
small star pattern**

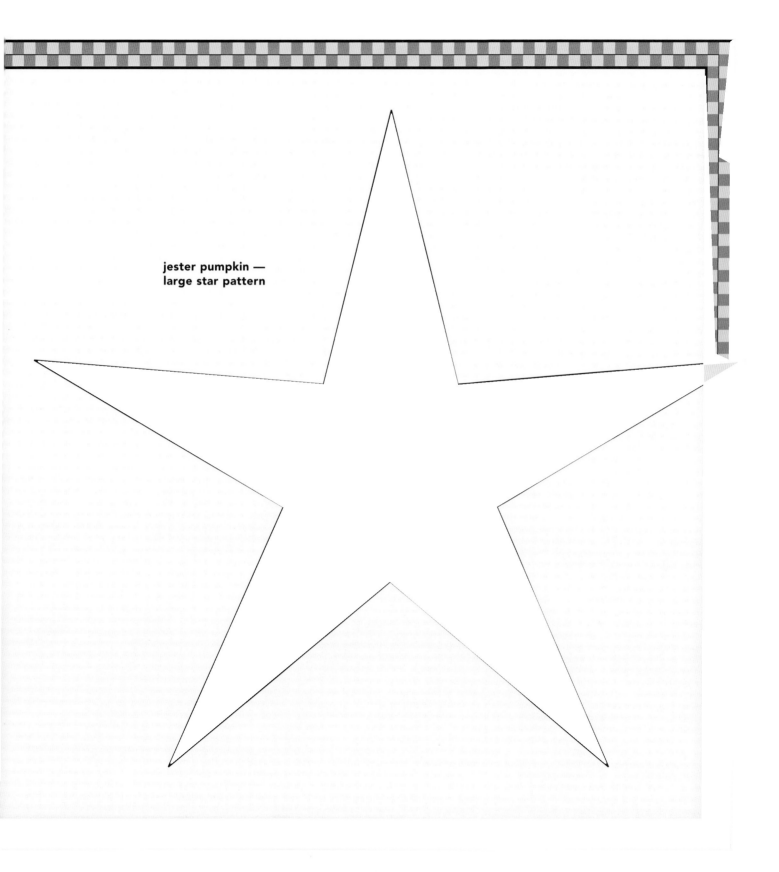

jester pumpkin —
large star pattern

friendly scarecrow

With an ear-to-ear grin and arms stretched out wide, this happy fellow adds a cheerful touch to your autumn decorating.

WHAT YOU'LL NEED

Tracing paper and pencil
Scissors
½ yard of tan evenweave fabric
Orange felt scrap
Embroidery floss in black, red,
  and yellow
Two 1½-inch blue buttons
15¾x11¼-inch piece of
  ¾-inch-thick board
Drill and ³⁄₁₆-inch drill bit
2-inch-long ³⁄₁₆-inch screw with
  flat head
36-inch-long ¾-inch-diameter
  dowel
24-inch-long ½-inch-diameter
  dowel
Acrylic paints in black, white,
  and lavender
½-inch-wide flat paintbrush
Ruler
Black permanent marker
Strapping tape
24-gauge wire
Child's size 5 purchased overalls,
  button-up shirt, and jacket
Fiberfill
15 inches of rope
Striped tie

Green and yellow fabric scraps
Pinking shears
Straw hat
Silk sunflowers
1 yard of ¾-inch-wide ribbon
Hot-glue gun and hot glue
Raffia in red and yellow
Powder blush

HERE'S HOW

1. Enlarge and trace the head and nose patterns, *pages 24–25,* onto tracing paper. Cut out. Use the head pattern to cut two pieces from tan fabric. Cut the nose from orange felt.
2. Using two plies of black embroidery floss, stitch the nose to the center of one face piece using small stitches. Use six plies of black embroidery floss and running stitches to create the curved part of the mouth. Make the short vertical lines using straight stitches. Sew on the button eyes using six plies of red embroidery floss.
3. Place the two head pieces, right sides together, and stitch using a ¼-inch seam allowance. Leave the neck area open. Turn right side out.

4. Cut a 5x28-inch piece from tan fabric, piecing if necessary. Sew the short ends together to make a continuous loop for the collar

(continued on pages 24–25)

ruffle. Use embroidery floss to run a gathering stitch ½ inch from one edge. Set aside.

5. Drill a hole through the center of the board and in one end of the large dowel.

6. Paint the large dowel black. When dry, use the handle end of the paintbrush to add white polka dots. Let the paint dry.

7. Use a pencil and ruler to draw a ¾-inch-wide border around the top of the board. Paint the center of the board lavender and the border and edge white. Let the paint dry. Mark off ¾-inch squares around the edge and border. Paint every other square black. Let the paint dry. Outline purple rectangle using black marker.

8. Screw the screw through the bottom of the base board. Continue screwing into the drilled dowel until the dowel is tight to the board.

9. Place the remaining dowel 6 inches below the top of the painted dowel, making a "t." Tape the two dowels together, winding in an "X" pattern. For added strength, wind wire over the tape and twist the ends together.

10. Using pinking shears, cut patches from green and yellow fabrics. Sew them on the overalls, painting motifs on them first, if desired. Let the paint dry. Begin dressing the scarecrow by putting on the shirt. Stuff the body with fiberfill. Add the overalls, stuffing the legs, leaving about 8 inches at the bottom. Tie the legs below the stuffing using rope. Put on the jacket (turning up the cuffs if needed), tucking a patch in one of the pockets, if desired. Colorful buttons can be used to replace dull buttons.

11. Use fiberfill to stuff the head. Slip the open end over the top of

the dowel. Tuck the fabric neck into the shirt collar.

12. With the gathering stitches up, slip the tan collar ruffle over the head. Pull the ends of the embroidery floss until it is snug to the neck. Knot the ends and trim the excess floss. Tie the necktie at the top of the ruffle.

13. Glue a sunflower to the top of the hat. Glue ribbon around the crown of the hat and tie a bow near the sunflower.

14. Tie small bundles of 12- to 16-inch pieces of red raffia in the center. Fold in half and glue inside the back and sides of the straw hat. Place on the head, adding hair until the desired look is achieved.

15. Stuff the pockets and ends of the sleeves with yellow raffia. A small sunflower can be placed in the lapel, if desired. Use powder blush to add color to the cheeks.

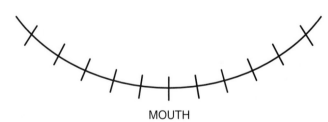

MOUTH

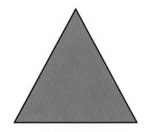

NOSE

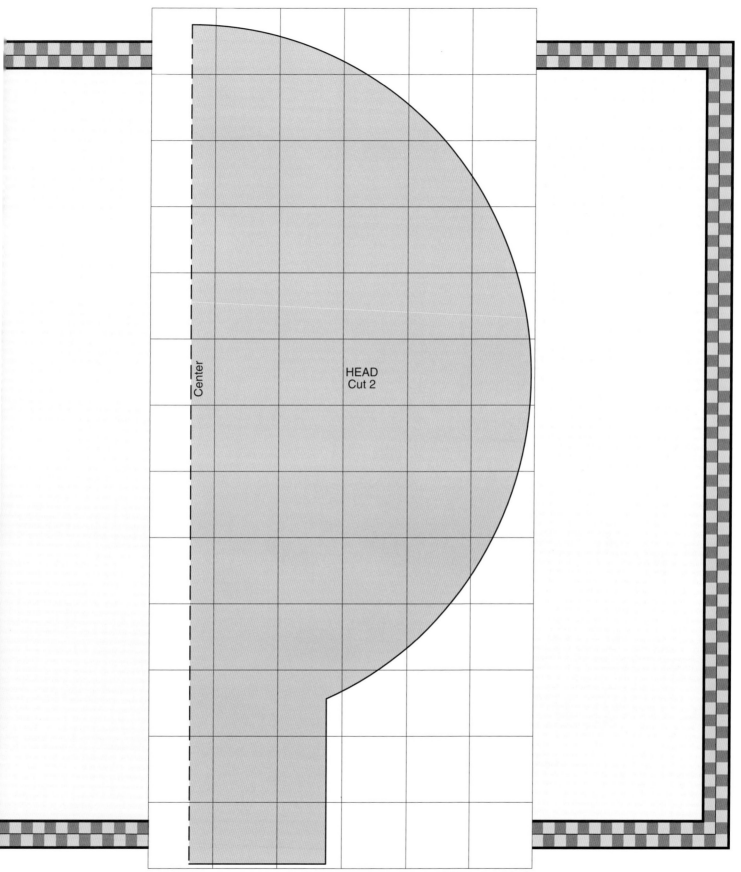

Center

HEAD
Cut 2

1 Square = 1 Inch

"boo" table mat

Add a "boo-tiful" touch to any table with this no-sew Halloween mat made of felt, rickrack, and a bit of paint.

WHAT YOU'LL NEED

Thick white crafts glue
Four 4x4-inch pieces of orange felt
1 sheet each of white, yellow, black, and orange felt
Two 4x9-inch pieces of black felt
Two 4x11-inch pieces of black felt
9x11-inch piece of royal blue felt
19x21-inch piece of yellow felt
Tracing paper
Pencil
White fabric marker
Scissors
White acrylic paint
Round paintbrush
2½ yards of ¼-inch-wide orange satin ribbon
2½ yards of large black rickrack

HERE'S HOW

1. Glue an orange felt square in the corner of the large yellow felt piece, 1 inch from the edges. Repeat with the remaining three orange felt squares.

2. Glue the black felt rectangles between the orange squares, butting the ends.

3. Glue the royal blue felt piece in the center of the yellow felt.

4. Trace the patterns, *pages 28–29*, onto tracing paper and cut out. Trace around the ghost faces and candy corn tips (six times) on the piece of white felt. Trace around the candy corn (six times) on the yellow felt. Trace around the large candy corn end (six times) on the orange felt. Trace around the star (twenty times) and moon (four times) on the black felt using a white fabric marker. Cut out the felt shapes.

5. Using the photograph, *above right*, as a guide, glue the ghost faces in place. Outline the faces by painting light rings around the shapes. Let the paint dry.

6. Glue the white and orange pieces atop the yellow candy corn shapes. Glue the candy corn shapes by the ghost faces as shown, *above right*.

7. Arrange and glue five of the stars and one of the moon shapes atop an orange corner square. Repeat for the remaining orange squares, arranging each corner differently, if desired.

8. Cut two 17-inch-long and two 19-inch-long pieces of orange ribbon. Glue the pieces in place around the royal blue center rectangle. Glue rickrack around the yellow felt edge, cutting and butting rickrack at the corners.

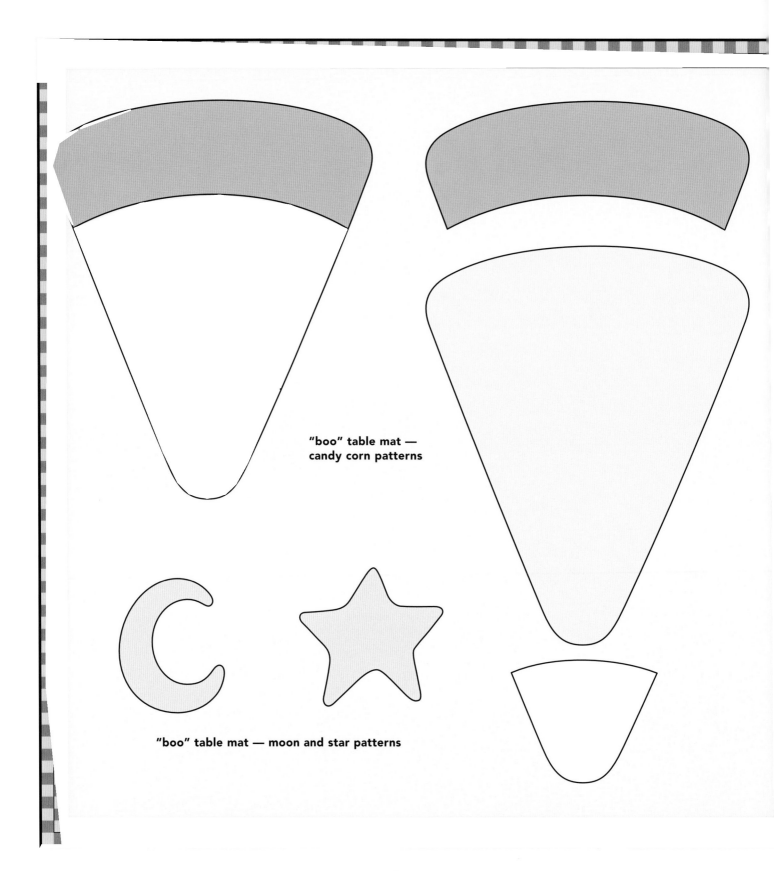

"boo" table mat —
candy corn patterns

"boo" table mat — moon and star patterns

"boo" table mat —
ghost face patterns

winter

 From the breathtaking sight of the first gentle snow to heartwarming gatherings with those you love, WINTER is a time of wonder, magic, and merriment. This chapter is filled with unique ideas to help you create an unforgettable season of joy for your family and friends. Join us as we share crafts to make and wear with pride, and trims to make your home shine brightly all winter long.

fancy figure skates

Transform scuffed-up leather skates into door decor that's as welcoming
as any holiday wreath.

WHAT YOU'LL NEED

Pair of girls' or women's
    figure skates
Paintbrushes
Acrylic paints in black,
    white, red, green, metallic
    green, blue, purple, and
    metallic yellow
Water-based varnish
White iridescent glitter
3 yards of ¼-inch-wide
    metallic gold ribbon
    for laces

(continued on pages 34–35)

HERE'S HOW

1. Remove the laces and clean the skates. Let the skates dry.

2. Slip the tongues out of the skates. Paint the tongues of the skates the desired color and let them dry. Tuck the tongues inside the skates.

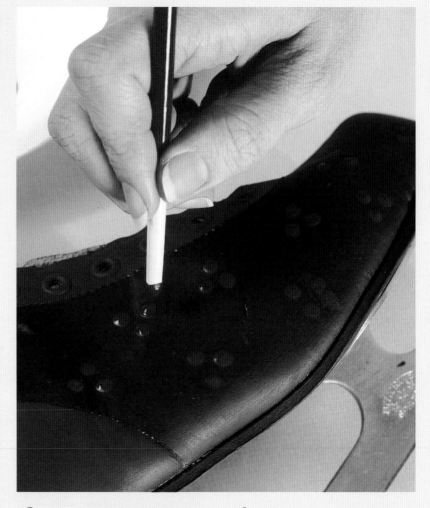

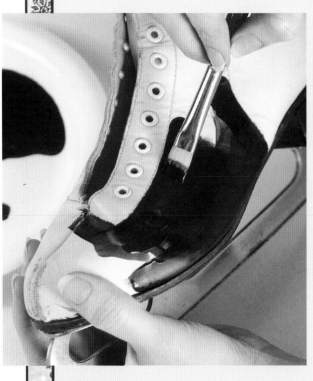

◀ **3.** Using the seams as guides, paint each section of the skates a solid color. Let the paint dry.

▲ **4.** Add holly berries by dipping the handle end of a paintbrush into red paint and dotting onto the surface three times as shown.

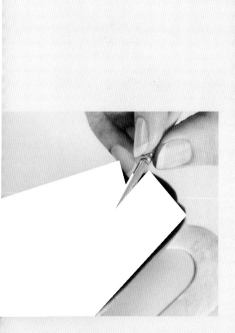

▲ **5.** Paint the green leaves by painting a zigzag, starting large and ending small.

▶ **6.** Paint little wrapped package motifs by painting solid squares and adding ribbons with a fine pointed paintbrush. Use a fine pointed brush to make stripes and lines on the packages as desired. Paint each of the grommets a different color. Paint red stripes along the sole. Let the paint dry.

◀ **7.** Coat everything with a clear coat of water-based varnish. After the varnish is thoroughly dry, coat the blades with varnish and sprinkle white iridescent glitter onto them. Let dry. Lace the skates with a generous length of gold ribbon.

winter warm-up chair

Come in from the cold and enjoy a steaming cup of cocoa while sitting on this whimsical chair that's as merry as the season itself.

WHAT YOU'LL NEED
Wooden chair
Sandpaper
White primer spray paint
Paintbrushes
Acrylic paints in blue, red, yellow,
   gold, white, black, olive green,
   and grass green
Snowflake stickers
Clear non-yellowing varnish
Fabric to cover the seat
Staple gun

HERE'S HOW
1. If the chair has an upholstered seat, remove it by unscrewing the screws underneath. Sand the surfaces to smooth any nicks or imperfections.

2. Spray two or three light coats of white primer on the chair's surface.
3. Begin painting the chair, using the structure lines and details of the chair as a guide for separating colors. Paint all of the surfaces a solid color first, then add the details. To paint stripes, use a good flat brush the width of your desired stripe. Add snowflake stickers where desired. Add small painted dots in between the snowflakes. To paint dots, dip the handle end

of the paintbrush in paint and dot it on the surface. Let all paint dry and seal with two to three coats of clear non-yellowing varnish.
4. Cover the chair seat with a coordinating fabric of your choice. Cut a piece of fabric at least 3½ inches larger all around than the seat. Place it over the seat and staple it on the back side in one corner. Staple the opposite corner pulling the fabric tightly as you staple. Continue in this manner until all sides are firmly stapled on the back. Secure the upholstered seat in place.

star-studded st. nick

Festively trimmed from head to toe, this merry Santa

is crafted using simple paper-folding techniques.

WHAT YOU'LL NEED

Electric drill and ¼-inch bit
6-inch-wide natural wooden base
Two 9-inch-long ¼-inch dowels
Thick white crafts glue
Tracing paper; pencil
Scissors
Rubber band
Red pencil
Medium-weight paper in brown,
   beige, black, dark green, lime
   green, and yellow
White drawing paper
Sheet of 80# red artist paper
Black slick fabric paint pen
Pinking shears
Large round paper punch
Blue acrylic paint; paintbrush
Star-shaped paper punch
Fine-tip permanent markers in red
   and black
12-inch-long small branch
Green moss and tiny acorns

HERE'S HOW

1. Drill two ¼-inch holes, angled slightly inward, in the center of the wooden base, 1¼ inches apart from each other. Glue a wooden dowel into each hole.

2. Trace all patterns, *pages 40–43,* onto tracing paper. Cut out patterns and transfer to the appropriate colors of paper. Cut out shapes.

3. *For shoes,* overlap the back tab and glue. Use black slick paint to add shoe laces. When dry, slip shoes over the wooden dowels.

4. *For legs,* roll each shape into a tube. Cut thin strips of black with pinking shears and glue on to make vertical stripes. Overlap the edges ¼ inch and glue. When dry, slip legs over dowels. Squeeze the tops of the legs together and wrap with a rubber band 2½ inches down from the top. Glue the back of each leg to the back of corresponding shoe.

5. *For coat,* paint the center front portion to create a diamond pattern. To create the pattern, draw diagonal lines and paint every other diamond blue. Outline the patterns with black paint pen. Overlap the front and back pieces and glue edges together. Slip coat over top of legs and slide down to top of rubber band. Add glue around top inside of coat.

6. *For cloak,* fan pleat a 1x25-inch strip of white paper. Open up and glue to bottom edge of cloak. Allow to dry. Glue dark green strips to front edges of cloak. Cut lime green strips using pinking shears and glue over the dark green strips. Using a star paper punch, punch out several stars from black paper. Glue to the cloak and add black marker dots to encircle each star. Wrap and glue top edge of

(continued on pages 40–43)

cloak around body tube, allowing bottom edge to flair out.

7. *For head,* draw eyes on center of piece with black felt pen. Roll the head into a tube and glue the edges. Glue top of nose to top edge of head between the eyes. Use red pencil to color the cheeks. Glue the side strips of the larger beard to the face. Apply glue to inside bottom edge of head tube and slide head over the legs that extend above the coat. Fringe bottom edge of hair shape. Glue top edge of hair to top edge of head, overlapping the front edge of the hair over the side strips of the beard. Glue the side strips of the smaller beard to the edge of the hair strip, causing the smaller beard to stand slightly away from the larger beard.

8. *For arms and sleeves,* glue gloves to end of each arm. Add a ½-inch-wide pleated cuff strip to bottom edge of each sleeve piece. Add a border of black paint dots just above cuff. Allow to dry. Use a paper punch to make dots to add to sleeve. Glue on dots and add red dots in the centers with red marking pen. Fold sleeve in half lengthwise. Slip a sleeve over an arm, lining up bottom edge of sleeve with end of arm. Glue the back ¾ inch of the sleeve around the arm. Repeat for other sleeve. Glue the center back section of the arm to the center back of the coat.

9. *For hat,* glue the tabs to the other side of the hat. Glue the tip

of the hat pieces together. Pleat a ½x6-inch strip of paper and glue around bottom edge of hat. Using a star-shaped paper punch, punch out black stars and glue onto the hat.

10. *For walking stick,* glue one star on the tip of the stick and the second star about 1½ inches below. Glue stick to hand and to the base. Surround the feet and stick with moss and tiny acorns.

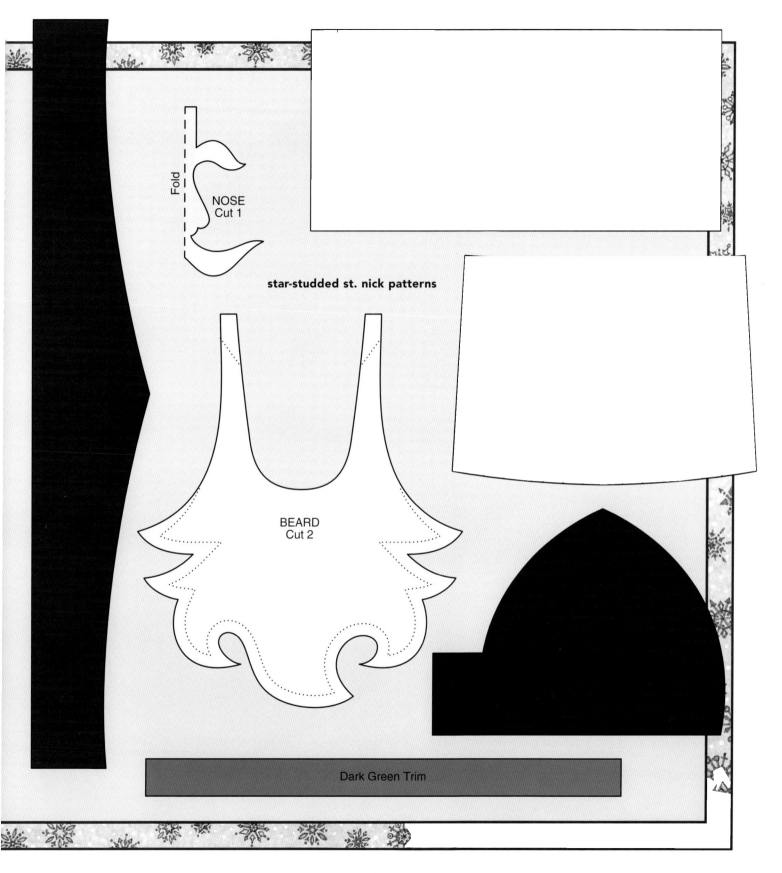

Fold

NOSE
Cut 1

star-studded st. nick patterns

BEARD
Cut 2

Dark Green Trim

41

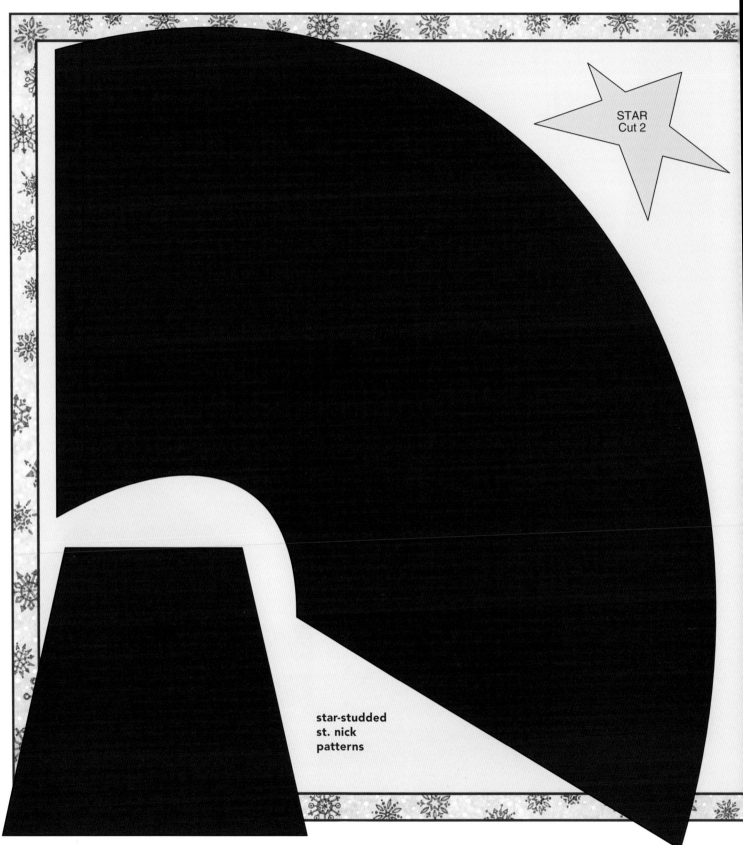

STAR
Cut 2

**star-studded
st. nick
patterns**

42

**star-studded
st. nick
patterns**

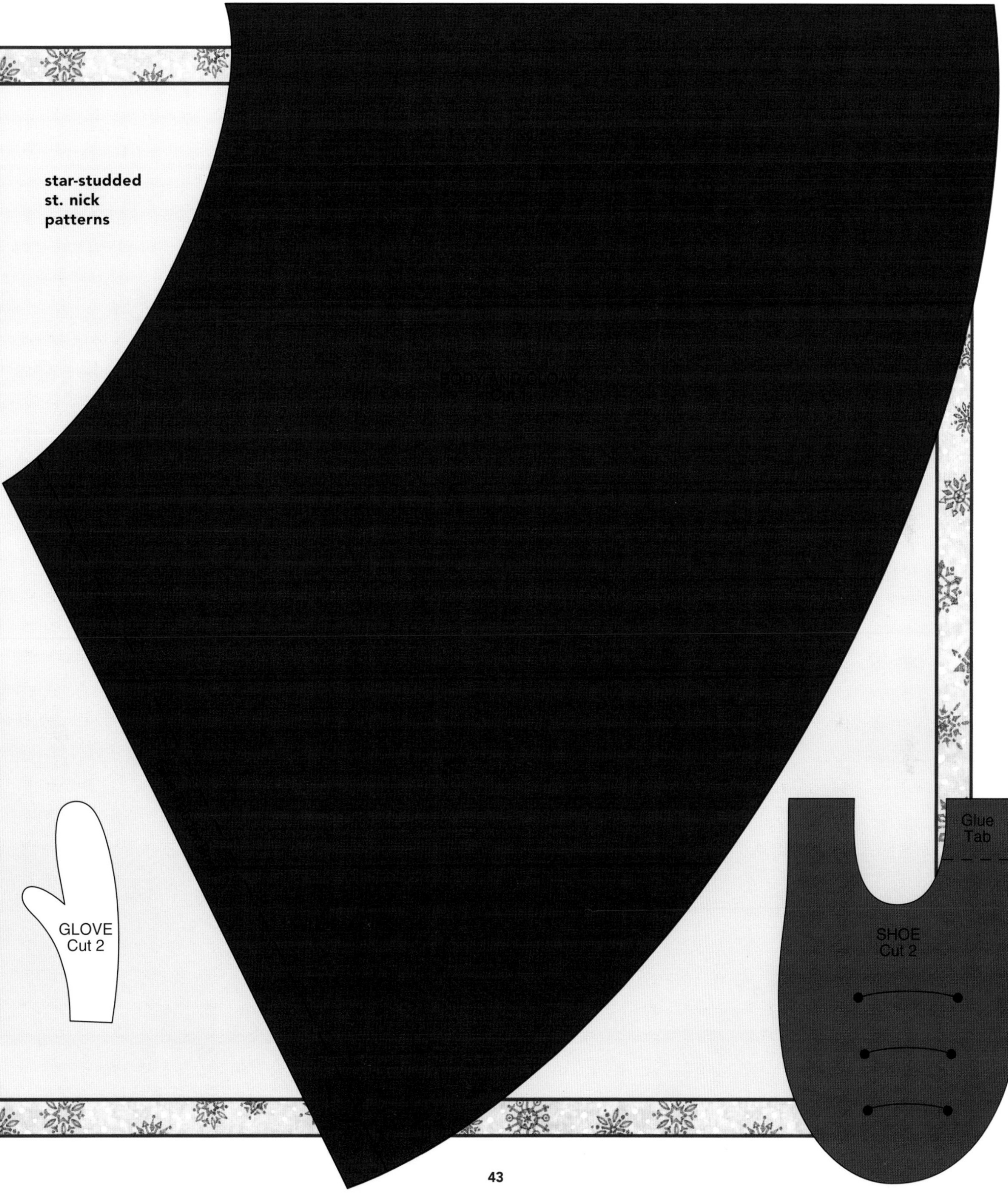

BODY AND CLOAK
Cut 1

GLOVE
Cut 2

SHOE
Cut 2

Glue
Tab

jolly
ornaments
& garlands

Create happy trims to grace the branches of your evergreen, or any spot in your holiday home. Instructions for all projects begin on page 47.

jolly snowman ornament

dancing
snowmen
garland

festive star
ornament

polka-dot
ornament

45

patchwork mitten ornament

jolly snowman ornament

See photograph, page 44.

WHAT YOU'LL NEED

Crayola Model Magic clay
Toothpick
2 black seed beads
Red, white, and green
  plastic-coated crafting wires
Paper clip
Two small 1½-inch-long sticks
Red Fimo clay
Thick white crafts glue
2 small green purchased
  pompons
Six ¼-inch colored buttons
Star charm
Beading wire
Small colored beads
Light pink acrylic paint
Paintbrush
Fine-tip black permanent marker
Ribbon

HERE'S HOW

1. Using a baseball-size piece of Model Magic, divide it into four equal parts. Roll one piece into a ball for the head. Combine the other three pieces and shape into an oval. Flatten one end for the base of the snowman.
2. Use the toothpick to poke two holes into the head for eyes. Put a black seed bead into each hole. Cut 3-inch lengths from each of the colored wires. Set the green wire aside. Twist the red and the white wires together to make the top of earmuffs. Form the twisted wire into a C-shape and push the ends into the sides of the snowman's head. Clip off a ½-inch U-shape from a paper clip. Push it into the back of the snowman's head for an ornament hanger.
3. Stick the toothpick into the top of the oval and push the head on the toothpick. Push a small stick into each side of the snowman's body for arms. Let the clay dry.
4. Form a pea-size piece of red Fimo clay into a small ball. Bake in oven as directed by the manufacturer. Remove from oven and let cool.
5. Glue the nose in the center of the face. Glue pompons over the ends of the twisted wires to resemble earmuffs. Glue buttons down the center of the body.
6. Thread the star charm onto the green wire. Secure the wire around the twisted wire as shown in photograph on *page 44.*
7. Cut a 5-inch length from beading wire. Make a tiny loop at one end to hold beads. Thread entire length with beads and form another loop at the end to secure. Drape the beaded wire over the snowman's arms.
8. Paint the cheeks using pink paint. Let the paint dry. Use a permanent marker to draw eyebrows and a mouth.
9. Thread the ribbon through the paper clip hanger.

dancing snowmen garland

See photograph, page 45.

WHAT YOU'LL NEED

Tracing paper; pencil
Scissors
White, black, and orange
  crafting foam
Thick white crafts glue
Acrylic paint in light pink
Paintbrush
Large black seed beads
Fine-tip black permanent marker
½-inch and ¼-inch green and red
  purchased pompons
Dental floss; sewing needle

HERE'S HOW

1. Trace the patterns, *page 48,* onto tracing paper and cut out. Trace around the patterns as many times as desired on the sheets of crafting foam and cut out the shapes.
2. Glue a black hat on each snowman's head. Glue the noses in the centers of the heads. Paint pink cheeks on each side of the nose. Glue seed bead eyes on either side of the nose. Use a marker to make a dotted smile on each snowman's face. Glue three small pompons on each snowman for buttons. Let the glue dry.
3. Cut a 36-inch-long piece of dental floss and thread through the

(continued on page 48)

needle. Thread a large green pompon on one end of floss and knot to secure. Thread on four more large pompons, alternating red and green.

4. To add a snowman on the garland, poke the needle through the front of the left hand. Bring the floss around the snowman's back and poke the needle through the back of the right hand. Continue

adding pompons and more snowmen in this manner.

festive star ornament
See photograph, page 45.

WHAT YOU'LL NEED
Purchased 4-inch-wide cardboard
  dimensional star

Acrylic paints in yellow, light
  orange, and red
¼-inch-wide flat paintbrush
Fine-tip black permanent marker
Ruler
Large safety pin
14-inch piece of 36-gauge
  copper wire
Large red and yellow seed beads
2 small red seed beads
¼-inch-wide red ribbon

**dancing snowmen
garland**

cherry fresh garland

HERE'S HOW

1. Paint the entire star yellow. Put a little light orange paint on the brush and paint the raised areas of the star. Let the paint dry.

2. Using a black marker and a ruler as a guide, draw a line around the star, ¼ inch from the edge. Paint red checks from the drawn line to the star edge approximately every ¼ inch. Let the paint dry.

3. Thread 6 inches of the wire with beads, alternating with red and yellow. To make holes to attach the beaded wire, push the safety pin through a star point, about ¼ inch from the tip. Skip a point and poke another hole on the next star point. Push each end of the wire through a hole in the star. Twist the ends around the handle of the paintbrush to secure. Glue a small red seed bead on each end of the wire.

4. Thread the ribbon through the beaded wire to hang.

polka–dot ornament

See photograph, page 45.

WHAT YOU'LL NEED

Round white ornament
Black glass paint
Pencil with round-tip eraser
24 inches of 1½-inch-wide black with white polka-dot satin ribbon
Thick white crafts glue
¼-inch-wide red ribbon

HERE'S HOW

1. To make the dots, dip the eraser end of a pencil into black paint and dot it on the surface. Make dots on one side and let the paint dry. Turn ornament over and add dots to the other side. Let dry.

2. Tie a bow with the wide ribbon. Glue it to the top of the ornament. Thread the narrow ribbon through the ornament loop and knot the ends.

patchwork mitten ornament

See photograph, page 46.

WHAT YOU'LL NEED

Waxed paper
Crayola Model Magic clay
Rolling pin; mitten cookie cutter
Drinking straw
Ruler
Fine-tip black permanent marker
Acrylic paints in dark green, bright gold, red, light sage green, brown, and white; paintbrush
Pencil with round-tip eraser
Toothpick
Two 16-inch-long pieces of ¼-inch-wide red and green striped ribbon

(continued on page 50)

HERE'S HOW

1. Tear off two pieces of waxed paper, each about 12 inches long. Place one on a flat working surface. Place a lemon-size piece of clay in the center of the waxed paper. Place the second piece of waxed paper on top of the clay and push down.

2. Use the rolling pin to flatten the clay evenly until it is about ¼ inch thick. Remove the top piece of waxed paper.

3. Cut the mitten shape with the cookie cutter. To make a hole at the top for hanging, insert the straw about ¼ inch from the mitten tip and remove. Let the mitten shape air dry as instructed by the manufacturer.

4. Use a ruler and fine-tip marker to divide the front of the mitten into three sections as shown on *page 46*. Paint the mitten tip with dark green. Paint the cuff section with white. Paint the thumb section with bright gold. Let the paint dry.

5. To make white dots on the dark green, dip the round eraser end of a pencil into white paint and dot on the surface as many times as desired. Let the paint dry. Add small red dots to the centers of the white dots by using the handle end of the paintbrush. Let the paint dry. Outline the white dots using the black marker.

6. Paint tiny triangles on the thumb section using light sage green. Add small brown trunks

to trees. Use the handle end of the paintbrush to add a white dot on the top of each tree and red dots between the trees. Dip a toothpick in red paint to make tiny dots encircling each larger red dot.

7. On the cuff section, paint thin red stripes about every ¼ inch. Paint wavy dark green lines between the stripes, adding tiny leaves on each side of the lines. Use gold to outline each red stripe. Let all of the paint dry. If desired, paint the other side of the mitten in the same manner.

8. Thread a ribbon through the hole for a hanger. Tie the remaining ribbon into a bow around the cuff.

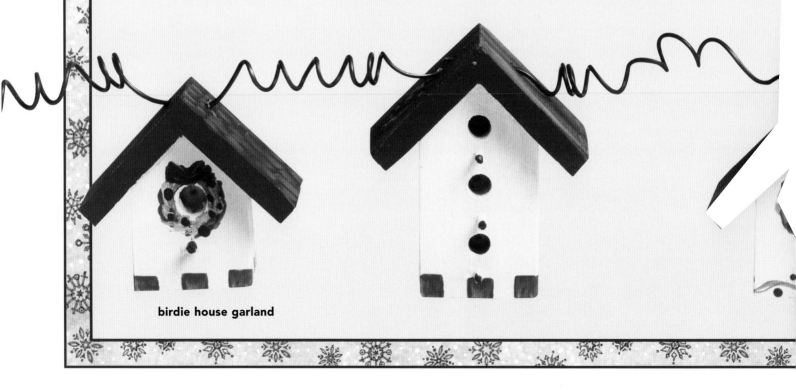

birdie house garland

cherry fresh garland

See photograph, page 49.

WHAT YOU'LL NEED

¾-inch wooden beads
Acrylic paints in black and white
Paintbrush
Red string
Artificial cherries on stems

HERE'S HOW

1. Paint half of the beads black and half white. Let the paint dry.
2. Using a length of string, tie a bead on one end. Thread on the remaining beads in the desired order. Tie on the last bead securely.
3. Use 12-inch lengths of string to tie pairs of cherries between the beads where desired.

birdie house garland

See photograph, below.

WHAT YOU'LL NEED

Electric drill with ¹⁄₁₆-inch bit
Purchased wooden birdhouses,
  1½ to 2 inches high
Scrap piece of board
Safety glasses
Acrylic paints in ivory, red,
  and green; paintbrush
16-gauge wire
Wire cutter
Pencil

HERE'S HOW

1. To drill a hole through a birdhouse, rest it on the scrap piece of board. Wearing safety glasses, drill a hole through the center of the roof, about ¼ inch below the peak. Drill holes through all of the birdhouses.
2. Paint the roofs red. Paint the rest of the birdhouses ivory. Let the paint dry.
3. Looking at the photograph, *below,* for inspiration, paint simple designs on each birdhouse, such as a wreath, checks, wavy lines, and dots. Let the paint dry.
4. Cut a 36-inch length of wire. To make small coils between birdhouses, wrap about 3 inches of wire around a pencil. Thread on a birdhouse and wrap another 3 inches of wire around a pencil. Repeat this process until the end of the wire is reached. Gently pull the wire apart to create uneven coils.

birdhouse bird feeder

Miniature birdhouses paint up quickly to become
the center attraction in this bird-beckoning seed holder.

WHAT YOU'LL NEED

Terra-cotta flower pot base about
  14 inches in diameter
Acrylic paints in grass green, lime
  green, black, white, red, yellow,
  purple, and blue
Paintbrush
4 small purchased birdhouses
  on dowels (available at crafts and
  discount stores)
White picket fence pieces
  purchased in crafts store
3½ x5-inch board
Drill with bit to match birdhouse
  stick thickness
Liquid Nails weatherproof glue
Birdseed

HERE'S HOW

1. Wash and dry terra-cotta pot
base. Paint the base with the
darker green. (You do not have
to paint the bottom.) Let the
paint dry.

2. Paint small stripes on the
outside rim of the base using
lime green and a flat brush about
¼ inch wide.
3. Paint each birdhouse a solid
color of choice. Paint the roofs and
sticks black. Add checks and dots
as desired. To make dots, dip the
handle end of the paintbrush in
white paint and dot onto the surface.
To paint white stripes, use a small
flat paintbrush.
4. Paint the picket fences white.
(If you cannot find these miniature
fences in a crafts store, you can
achieve the same look by gluing
popsicle sticks together. To cut
pointed ends on the top pickets, use
a scissors and cut away from the long
end of the stick.)
5. Decide how you want the four
birdhouses positioned and mark
holes on the small block of wood.
Carefully drill holes in the wood.
6. Glue all the pieces together
using weatherproof glue. Glue the
board to the pot base. Insert the

birdhouse sticks into the board.
(You may want to cut the sticks to
different lengths so that the
heights are staggered.) Glue the
picket fence to the edge of the
board. Fill the feeder with birdseed.

elegant floral stocking

Special surprises peek through the delicate fabric of this lovely 19-inch stocking that you'll be proud to hang for Santa to fill.

WHAT YOU'LL NEED

Tracing paper
Pencil
Scissors
½ yard of green sheer and
 satin stripe fabric
½ yard of multi sheer and
 satin stripe fabric
Five to six 2½-inch-long
 silver/gray double stamens
 for each flower
Three to five 4-inch-long
 red/green stamens for
 each flower
3 stems purchased satin
 leaves with three 2-inch
 leaves per stem
4x4-inch piece of stiff
 interfacing
1¼ yards of 1½-inch-wide pink
 ribbon for bow

HERE'S HOW

1. Enlarge the stocking pattern, *page 57*, onto tracing paper and cut out. Place the pattern crosswise on the green fabric. Cut two. To make a French seam in the stocking, place the wrong sides together. Stitch sides and bottom with ⅛-inch seam. Turn to wrong side and stitch seam again ¼ inch. Narrow hem the top edge.
2. Turn the cuff down 4 inches. Make a narrow fabric loop for hanging and stitch along center back seam.
3. For large flowers cut bias strips of multi sheer fabric 4x28 inches. Fold in half lengthwise, wrong sides facing. Machine-stitch gathering threads along raw edges (see Diagram 1 on *page 56*). Turn down right end at a right angle so that fold matches at gathering as shown in Diagram 2. Pleat and roll turned down end clockwise one

(continued on pages 56–57)

turn to form flower center as shown in Diagram 3. Secure center with a few hand stitches to a piece of interfacing.

4. Fold five silver/gray stamens in half and stitch to center of flower. Poke small hole in interfacing at flower center. Slip five red/green stamens into hole end and handstitch on back. Trim ends of stamens. Gather remaining bias fabric and twist around center counterclockwise securing to interfacing, tapering and pleating end. Trim the extra interfacing from the flower and fabric tail from flower center.

5. For small flower, repeat steps for large flower, cutting bias fabric 3x26 inches. Use silver/gray and red/green stamens. Make two large and one small flower. Position flowers and leaves onto stocking and cuff according to the photograph, *page 55.* Make bow from ribbon and add to back seam.

diagram 1

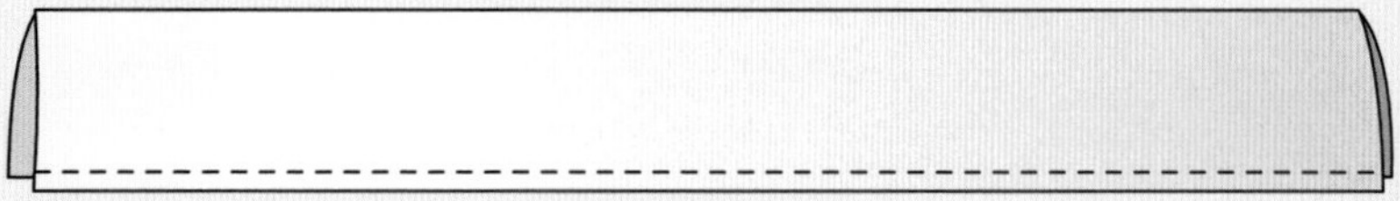

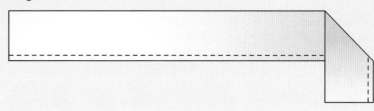

diagram 2

diagram 3

elegant floral stocking flower diagrams

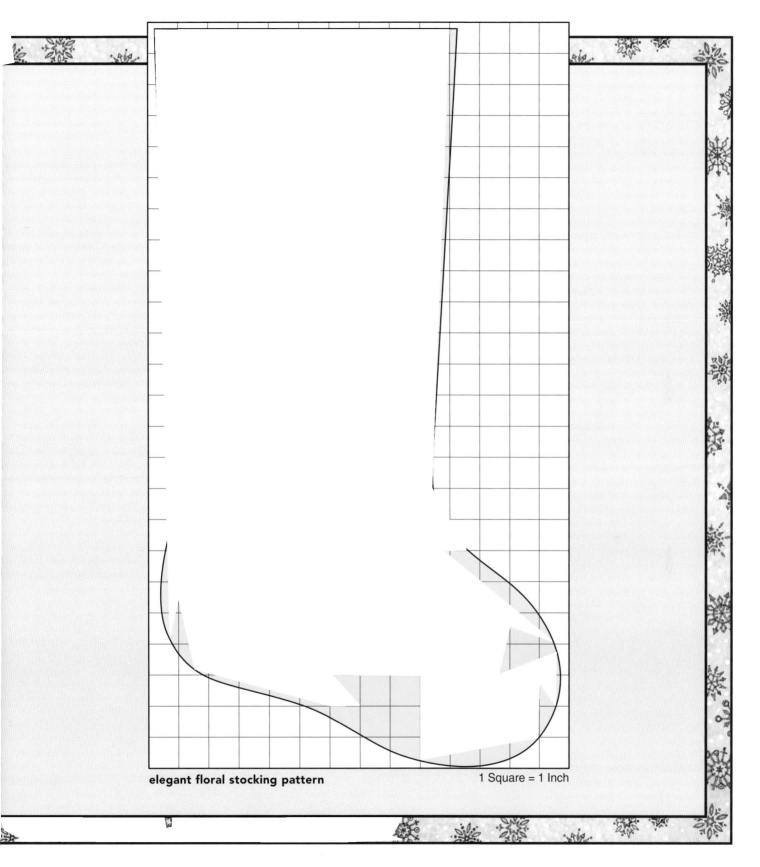

elegant floral stocking pattern

1 Square = 1 Inch

winter sparkle bow

Welcome visitors into your home with a wreath that's topped with a one-of-a-kind bow that is sure to start friendly conversation flowing.

WHAT YOU'LL NEED
Tracing paper and pencil
Scissors
Foam-core board
Acrylic paints in white and black
Paintbrush
Thick white crafts glue
String of red beads
Jewelry, buttons, and beads
  in pairs
Black cord trim
Metal picture hanging hook
Liquid Nails adhesive

HERE'S HOW
1. Enlarge and trace the bow pattern, *below right*, onto tracing paper, cut it out, and trace it onto foam-core board. Cut out the bow shape. Paint the entire bow shape black. Using the pattern as a guide, draw in the inside bow lines with a light pencil.
2. Outline the edges of the bow design with a generous amount of glue. Position red beads onto this line to form the outlines. Spread a generous amount of glue on areas to be jeweled. Work with jewelry in a symmetrical manner so that each half looks the same or similar. For example, when using a pair of earrings, place one in the upper left corner of the bow and place the other in the upper right corner of the bow. Continue to add jewelry, buttons, and beads until the surface is filled. If there are small uncovered areas, they can be filled with tiny seed beads.
3. Trim the side edge with black cord trim. Apply glue to the edge of bow shape and apply cord. Let the bow dry.
4. Glue a hook to the back of the bow using Liquid Nails. Allow it to dry overnight. Attach the bow to a fresh wreath, adding ornaments, if desired.

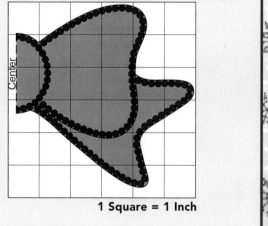

Center

1 Square = 1 Inch

mother-daughter sweater set

Add spunk to your wardrobe (and a little girl's, too)
with these comfy button-trimmed wearables.

child's button pullover sweater

Directions are for a child's size 2. Changes for size 4 and size 6 follow in parentheses. Finished chest size = 28(30, 32) inches.

WHAT YOU'LL NEED
Patons Look At Me Baby Sport
  yarn, 60% acrylic/40% nylon
  (1¾-oz./50 gm. skein): 4(5, 5)
  skeins of black (6364) and for all
  sizes, 1 skein of white (6351)
Size 5 circular knitting needle or
  size needed to obtain gauge
  (24-inch length and 16-inch length)
Tapestry needle
⅝-inch-diameter buttons; 6 green,
  6 yellow, and 4 red
One ring-type stitch marker
Stitch holders

Gauge: In Body Pattern, 24 sts and
  37 rows = 4 inches.

Abbreviations:

beg	beginning
bet	between
BO	bind off
CO	cast on
cont	continue
dec	decrease
inc	increase
k	knit
p	purl
pat	pattern
psso	pass slipped stitch over
rem	remaining
rep	repeat
rnd(s)	round(s)
rs	right side
sl	slip
WS	wrong side
wyif	with yarn in front
wyib	with yarn in back
yb	yarn back
yf	yarn forward
yo	yarn over

Note: The pullover is worked in rounds using a circular needle until completion of the plaid border. While working the plaid pattern, keep the wrong-side strands loose when slipping each 5-stitch group. When instructed to sl 1 or sl 5 (wyif or wyib), slip the stitch or stitches purlwise. Twist strands at beginning of each rnd to prevent holes.

HERE'S HOW
LOWER BORDER
With larger circular needle and black, CO 168(180, 188) sts. Place a marker to indicate beg of rnd.

(continued on page 62)

Keeping sts untwisted, join.

Rnd 1: * K 2, p 2; rep from * around.

Rnds 2–3: Rep Rnd 1.

Rnd 4: * K 2 black sts, k 2 white sts; rep from * around.

Rep Rnd 4 for 9 more times. K 1 black rnd, inc 2(0, 2) sts evenly spaced = 170(180, 190) sts.

FOR PLAID PATTERN

Rnd 1: With white, *(sl 1 wyif, sl 1 wyib) twice, sl 1 wyif, k 5; rep from * around.

Rnd 2: With black, (k 5, sl 5 wyib) around.

Rnd 3: With white, * (sl 1 wyib, sl 1 wyif) twice, sl 1 wyib, k 5 ; rep from * around.

Rnd 4: Rep Rnd 2.

Rnds 5, 6, 7, 8: Rep rnds 1–4.

Rnd 9: Rep Rnd 1.

Rnd 10: With black, * k5, (sl 1 wyif, sl 1 wyib) twice, sl 1 wyif; rep from * around.

Rnd 11: With white, (sl 5 wyib, k 5) around.

Rnd 12: With black, * k 5, (sl 1 wyib, sl 1 wyif) twice, sl 1 wyib; rep from * around.

Rnd 13: Rep Rnd 11.

Rnds 14, 15, 16, 17: Rep rnds 10–13.

Rnd 18: Rep Rnd 10.

Rep rnds 1–18 twice; then rep rnds 1–9 again. K 1 rnd black, adjusting number of stitches on last two sizes to (182, 194); turn.

BACK: P 85(91, 97); place rem 85(91, 97) sts onto holders for front.

Body Pattern, Row 1 (RS); K 1, * p 2, yb, sl 1 purlwise, yf; rep from * across, ending last rep p 2, k 1.

Row 2: P 1, * k 2, p 1; rep from * across.

Rep rows 1-2 of Body Pat until piece measures 15(17½, 19) inches from beg, ending with a RS row. BO loosely in body pattern. FRONT: Work as for Back to 12½(15, 16½) inches from beg, ending with a WS row.

Neck Shaping: In est pat, work 34(36, 38) sts; join a new strand and BO center 17(19, 21) sts; work to end of row. Working sides separately and at the same time, BO at each neck edge 5 sts once, 3 sts once and 2 sts once. Work on rem 24(26, 28) sts to same length as Back, ending with a RS row. BO loosely in pattern.

SLEEVE (make two): Beginning at lower edge with circular needle and black, CO 38(42, 46) sts. NOTE: Do not join; sleeves will be worked back and forth on the circular needle.

Row 1 (WS): P 1, k 2; (p 2, k 2) across, ending p 3.

Row 2: K 3; (p 2, k 2) across, ending p 2, k 1.

Row 3: Rep Row 1.

For Striped Border:

Row 1 (RS): K 3 black sts, * k 2 white sts, k 2 black sts; rep from *

across, ending last rep k 2 white sts, k 1 black st.

Row 2: P across in color pat.

Rep rows 1-2 for 6 times more. K 1 row black, inc 4(10, 6) sts evenly spaced = 42(52, 52) sts. P 1 row black.

For Plaid Pattern:

Row 1 (RS): With white, k 1; * (sl 1 wyif, sl 1 wyib) twice, sl 1 wyif, k 5; rep from * across, ending last rep k 6. SL STS TO OTHER END OF NEEDLE.

Row 2 (RS): With black, k 1; * k 5, sl 5 wyib; rep from * across, ending last rep k 1; TURN.

Row 3 (WS): With white, p 1, * p 5, (sl 1 wyif, sl 1 wyib) twice, sl 1 wyif; rep from * across, ending p 1. Sl sts to other end of needle.

Row 4 (WS): With black, p 1; * sl 5 wyif, p 5; rep from * across, ending last rep with p 6; turn.

Rows 5, 6, 7, 8, and 9: Rep rows 1, 2, 3, 4, and 1.

Row 10 (RS): With black, k 1; * k 5, (sl 1 wyif, sl 1 wyib) twice, sl 1 wyif; rep from * across, ending k 1; turn.

Row 11 (WS): With white, p 1; * p 5, sl 5 wyif; rep from * across, ending p 1. Sl sts to other end of needle.

Row 12 (WS): With black, p 1; * (sl 1 wyif, sl 1 wyib) twice, sl 1 wyif, p 5; rep from * across, ending last rep, p 6; turn.

Row 13 (RS): With white, k 1; * sl 5 wyib, k 5; rep from * across,

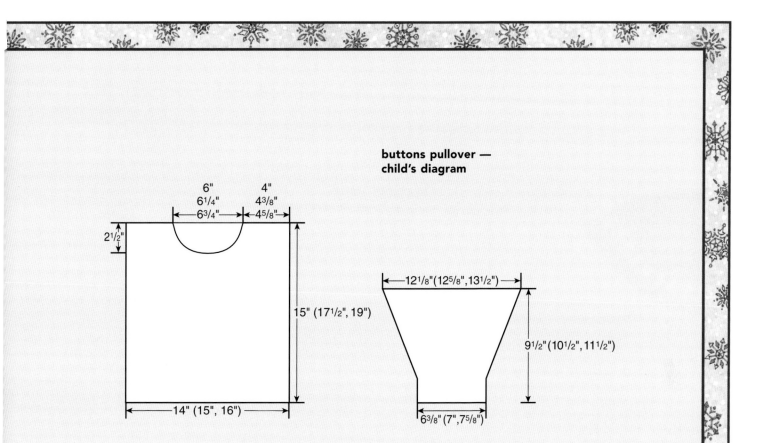

**buttons pullover —
child's diagram**

6"
6¼"
6¾"
4"
4⅜"
4⅝"
2½"
15" (17½", 19")
14" (15", 16")

12⅛"(12⅝",13½")
9½"(10½",11½")
6⅜" (7",7⅝")

ending last rep k 6. Sl sts to other end of needle.

Rows 14, 15, 16, 17, and 18: Rep rows 10, 11, 12, 13, and Row 10 again.

For Upper Sleeve; p 1 row with black, inc 7(6, 9) sts evenly spaced = 49(58, 61) sts. Work body pat as for Back for 4 rows. Keeping first and last sts in st st for selvage edge, and including new sts into body pat, inc 1 st each edge now, and then every 4th row until there are 73(76, 81) sts. Work even to

9½(10½, 11½) inches from beg, ending with a RS row. BO loosely in pat.

FINISHING: Sew shoulder seams. Place markers 6(6½, 7) inches each side of shoulder seams. Set in sleeves between markers. Join underarm and side seams.

Neckband: With the RS facing using shorter circular needle and black, beg at shoulder seam, pick up and k 92(96, 100) sts evenly spaced around neck. Place a

marker to indicate beg of rnd. K 1 rnd.

Rnds 2–5: (K 2 black, k 2 white) around.

Rnds 6–13: K around with black. BO loosely with black.

Turn neckband to inside of garment and whipstitch in place. Sew three buttons onto each shoulder evenly spaced and using one each of red, green, and yellow. Sew five buttons onto each sleeve just above the plaid section, alternating colors and spacing evenly.

adult button vest and hat

Directions are for a size small. Changes for medium, large, and extra-large follow in parentheses. Finished bust size = 36(38¾, 41½, 44) inches. Finished length = 18(18½, 19, 19½) inches.

WHAT YOU'LL NEED

Patons DECOR, 75% acrylic/25% wool yarn (210-yard./3½-oz./100-gm. skein): for vest and hat 3(3, 4, 5) skeins black (1603) and one skein white (1601)

Size 7 circular needle or size needed to obtain recommended gauge, 24-inch-length

Size 5 circular needle, 16-inch length

Twelve ⅝-inch-diameter buttons; four each of red, yellow, and green

Yarn needle; stitch holders

One ring-type stitch marker

Size 4/E (3.5 mm) aluminum crochet hook

GAUGE: In Body Pattern with larger needle, 22 sts = 5 inches; 29 rows = 4 inches.

Note: The vest is worked in rounds using a circular needle until completion of the plaid border. While working the plaid pattern, keep the wrong-side strands loose when slipping each 5-stitch group. When instructed to sl 1 or sl 5 (wyif or wyib), slip the stitch or stitches purlwise. Twist strands at the beginning of each rnd to prevent holes.

HERE'S HOW

Beginning at lower edge with larger circular needle and black, CO 160(168, 180, 188) sts. Place marker to indicate beg of rnd. Keeping sts untwisted, join and k 1 rnd. Work Lower Border as for child's pullover, k 1 rnd black, inc 0(2, 0, 2) sts = 160(170, 180, 190) sts. Work Plaid Pat as for child's pullover, adjusting number of sts to 158(170, 182, 194); TURN.

BACK: With black, p 79(85, 91, 97); place rem sts onto holders for front. Work Body Pat as for child's pullover until piece measures 8(8½, 8½, 8½) inches from beg.

Armhole Shaping: Keeping to est pat, BO 6 sts at the beg of the next 2 rows; then BO 3 sts at the beg of the next 2 rows = 61(67, 73, 79) sts. Keeping first and last st in st st for selvage edge, work even to 17(17½, 18, 18½) inches from beg, ending with a WS row.

Neck Shaping: Work first 14(16, 18, 20) sts; place center 33(35, 37, 39) sts onto a holder for back neck; join a new strand of black and work rem sts. Working sides separately and at the same time, cont est pat, dec 1 st at each neck edge once. When piece measures 18(18½, 19, 19½) inches from beg, ending with a RS row, BO rem 13(15, 17, 19) sts for each shoulder.

FRONT: Return sts to needle and p 1 row with black. Work as for Back until piece measures 15(15½, 16, 16½) inches from beg.

Neck Shaping: Work first 22(24, 26, 28) sts; place center 17(19, 21, 23) sts onto a holder for front neck; join a new strand of black and work rem sts. Working sides separately and at the same time, BO at each neck edge 5 sts once, 3 sts once, and 1 st once. Work even on rem 13(15, 17, 19) sts to same length as Back, ending with a RS row. BO loosely for each shoulder.

FINISHING: Join shoulder and side seams (above the plaid borders).

Armband: With the RS facing using smaller needle and black, pick up and k 110 (110, 116, 122) sts evenly spaced around armhole, beg at lower seam. Work 5 rnds of k 1, p 1 ribbing. BO in ribbing.

Neckband: With the RS facing using smaller needle and black beg at shoulder seam, pick up and k 96(100, 104, 108) sts evenly spaced around neck including sts from holders. Place marker for beg of rnd; join and k 1 rnd. Rnd 2: * K 2 black, k 2 white; rep from * around. Rep Rnd 2 for 3 times more. With black, k 8 rnds. BO loosely, knitwise. Turn band to inside of vest and sew in place.

**buttons vest —
adult diagram**

8"　　　　3"
8 3/8"　　　3 1/2"
8 7/8"　　　3 7/8"
9 3/8"　　4 3/8"

3"

10" (10", 10 1/2", 11")

8" (8 1/2", 8 1/2", 8 1/2")

18" (19 3/8", 20 3/4", 22")

Lower Edging: With the RS facing using crochet hook, join black with a sl st at one side. Ch 1, work 158 (170, 182, 194) sc around. Sl st in each sc around, skipping 15 sc at even intervals. At end, fasten off.

Alternating colors, sew six buttons along center front at even intervals.

HAT

Using black and size 7 needles, CO 106 sts. Working back and forth for entire hat, p 1 row, k 2 rows. Work striped border as for child's sleeve for 6 rows. With black, k 3 rows. Beg with a p row, work in st st for 1 inch, ending with a WS row and dec 1 st = 105 sts.

Hat Shaping: K 9, (sl 1 st knitwise, k2tog, psso = 2-st dec made); * k 18, make a 2-st dec; rep

from * across, ending last rep k 9.
Row 2: P 95 sts.
Rows 3–4: Work in st st.
Row 5: K 8; * 2-st dec, k 16; rep from * across, ending 2-st dec, k 8.
Rows 6–8: Work st st on 85 sts.
Row 9: K 7; * 2-st dec, k 14; rep from * across, ending 2-st dec, k 7.
Rows 10–12: Work st st on 75 sts.
Row 13: K 6; * 2-st dec, k 12; rep from * across, ending 2-st dec, k 6.
Rows 14–16: Work st st on 65 sts.

Crown: K 2 rows. P 1 row, dec 1 st = 64 sts.
Row 20: (K 6, k2tog) across.
Row 21: P 56.
Row 22: (K 5, k2tog) across.
Row 23: P 48.
Row 24: (K 4, k2tog) across.
Row 25: P 40.
Row 26: (K 3, k2tog) across.

Row 27: P 32.
Row 28: (K 2, k2tog) across.
Row 29: P 24.
Row 30: (K2tog) across = 12 sts. Break yarn, leaving a 12-inch tail. Thread tail into yarn needle and back through rem 12 sts. Pull up to close opening. Wait to join seam until lower edging is added.

Edging: With the RS facing using black and size 7 needle, pick up and k 106 sts along lower edge. P 1 row, inc 1 st = 107 sts. For picot edge, BO 2 sts; * slip rem st on right-hand needle back to left-hand needle, CO 2 sts, BO 4 sts; rep from * across and fasten off rem st.

With saved tail, join the back seam. Alternating colors, sew remaining buttons onto crown of hat.

cheery cherry mittens

Sporting appliquéd imitation-suede cherries,

these fancy sew-them-yourself mitts will keep

your fingers warm all winter long.

WHAT YOU'LL NEED

Tracing paper; pencil; scissors
½ yard of gold polar fleece
½ yard of lining fabric
Fusible web paper
4x4-inch pieces of Ultrasuede:
    two shades of red, two shades of
    green, and brown
Embroidery floss in red, green,
    and brown
28 faceted black 4mm beads
20 inches of ¼-inch-wide elastic
¼ yard of red corduroy
¾ yard of 2-inch-wide white fur

HERE'S HOW

1. Enlarge and trace the mitten pattern, *page 69*, onto tracing paper and cut out. Cut shapes from polar fleece and lining fabric (reversing the shapes for the opposite mitten).
2. Trace the cherry, stem, and leaf patterns onto the paper side of fusible web (reversing one set). Cut out shapes, leaving a ¼-inch margin, and fuse to Ultrasuede following the manufacturer's instructions. Cut out Ultrasuede appliqués.
3. Using a press cloth, fuse the cherries, leaves, and stems to mitten as shown. Buttonhole stitch around the appliquéd pieces using three plies of matching embroidery floss. Add stem stitches to leaf centers. Add straight-stitch highlights to the cherries.
4. Sew beads around cherry motifs.
5. Stitch mitten seams with right sides facing using a ¼-inch seam allowance. Stitch the thumb gusset around the curved edge from A to B. Stitch the inner seam of thumb and palm, tapering to a point at A. Machine-zigzag over the elastic stretched on the wrong side of the palm/thumb, 3 inches down from the top edge. Trim excess elastic.
6. Stitch mitten palm to back along side and finger curve. Turn right side out.

7. Repeat for the lining, leaving an opening for turning in side seam.
8. Cut two cuffs from the corduroy, each 6½x6½ inches. Stitch ends of cuff together. Press seams open. Fold cuff in half with wrong sides facing and matching raw edges.
9. Ease-stitch along the top edge of the cuff and baste to the mitten.
10. Slip mitten into lining, matching side seams and thumb. Stitch top edge. Slip-stitch opening in lining closed. Tuck lining into mitten and turn cuff down. Sew fur trim to cuff.

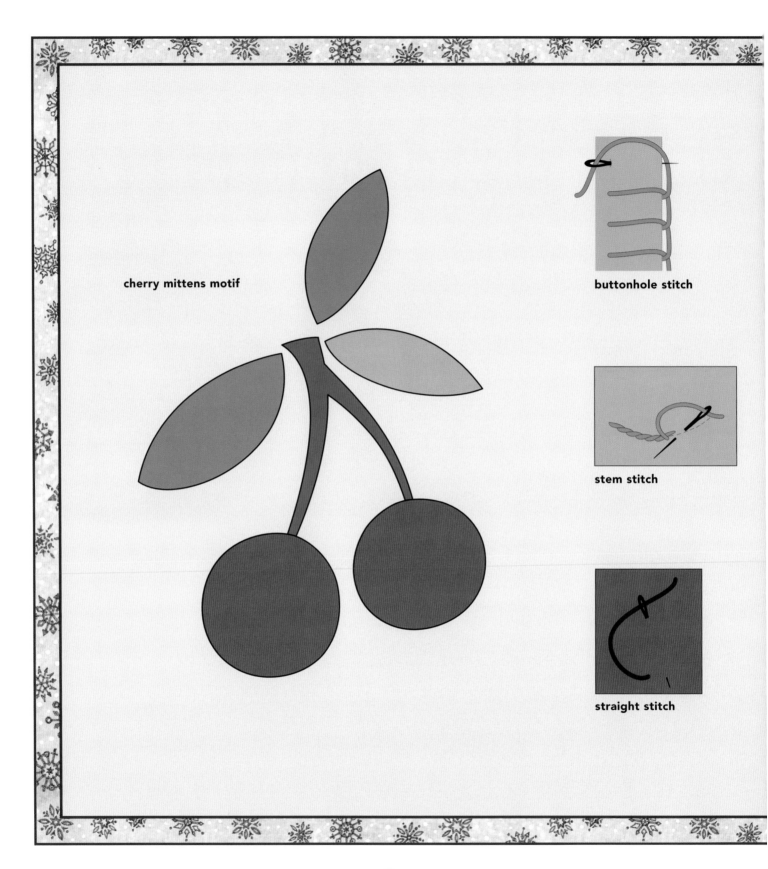

cherry mittens motif

buttonhole stitch

stem stitch

straight stitch

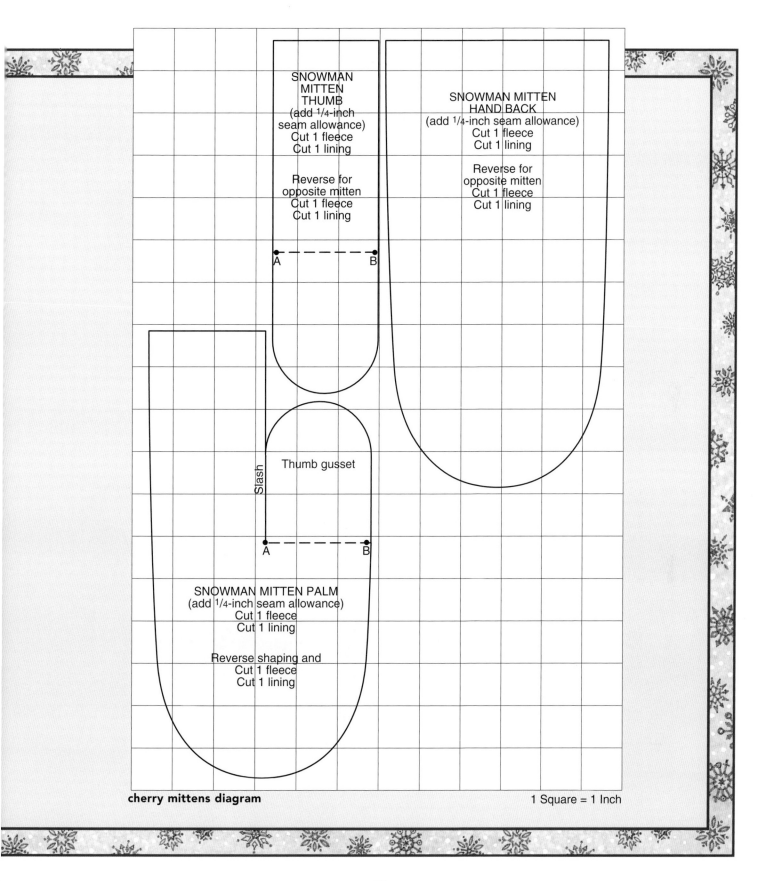

SNOWMAN
MITTEN
THUMB
(add 1/4-inch
seam allowance)
Cut 1 fleece
Cut 1 lining

Reverse for
opposite mitten
Cut 1 fleece
Cut 1 lining

A   B

SNOWMAN MITTEN
HAND BACK
(add 1/4-inch seam allowance)
Cut 1 fleece
Cut 1 lining

Reverse for
opposite mitten
Cut 1 fleece
Cut 1 lining

Slash

Thumb gusset

A   B

SNOWMAN MITTEN PALM
(add 1/4-inch seam allowance)
Cut 1 fleece
Cut 1 lining

Reverse shaping and
Cut 1 fleece
Cut 1 lining

cherry mittens diagram

1 Square = 1 Inch

spring

The colors are vivid, the scents are so sweet—it must be SPRING! As the season's blooms come poking through the soil, what a renewing time for those of us who love to craft! Just when you wondered what to do with an old watering can or how to add pizzazz to your Eastertime gatherings, this fun-filled chapter leads the way.

mother's suitcase

From children's artwork and special letters from friends to newspaper clippings and travel memorabilia, this decoupaged suitcase will hold many of mom's favorite treasures.

WHAT YOU'LL NEED
Old suitcase
Acrylic paints in ivory, peach, and
  light peach; paintbrush
Scissors
Cards, wrapping paper, or any
  pretty decorative paper to cut out
Paper doilies
Lace or braided trim
Mod Podge decoupage medium
Measuring tape
Wrapping paper, optional
Spray adhesive
Peach-colored satin
¼-inch foam padding
Tag board or card stock
Masking tape
Thick white crafts glue

HERE'S HOW
1. Begin with a clean suitcase. Paint the handle ivory. Paint both sides a light peach. Paint the edges the darker peach. Let the seams on the suitcase trim be a guide for painting. Let all surfaces dry and add a second coat if needed.

2. Cut out motifs from cards or other items to be decoupaged. Cut out pieces from doilies or use them whole. Plan and arrange all items to be used on the suitcase before beginning to decoupage. The papers may overlap for interest.
3. Paint the back of each item with a generous coat of decoupage medium before placing it onto the suitcase. Continue this process until all items are in place. Add lace or braided trim to the edges of the suitcase, if desired. When all cutouts are in place, coat entire suitcase with two more coats of decoupage, allowing it to dry between coats.

To cover the inside
You may cover the inside of the suitcase to complement the outside. This may take some measuring, but it gives a very nice finished look.
1. Using a measuring tape, measure each panel on the inside of the suitcase. Combine more

than one panel when possible, to avoid too many seams. Cut wrapping paper to these sizes. Use spray adhesive to affix the wrapping paper to the inside of the suitcase.
2. To create a padded satin insert, measure the suitcase bottom. Using spray adhesive, affix the foam padding to a piece of tag board or card stock paper larger than the area to be covered. Cut to the size measured, cutting through the foam and card stock. Cut a piece of satin about 2 inches larger all around than the prepared foam padding. Carefully place the smooth ironed piece of satin over the foam and tape to the back side of the card stock. Tape one side, then the opposite side, keeping satin smooth and taut but not too tight as to bend the card stock. When all edges are taped, coat the back (taped side) with a generous coat of crafts glue and place in the bottom of the suitcase.

eggs with character

These adorable characters will bring personality plus to the table when nestled in with brown or solid-dyed eggs.

WHAT YOU'LL NEED

Eggs
Toothpick
Pencil
Acrylic paints in red, yellow, blue, white, black, and pink; paintbrush
Scissors
Tracing paper
Crafting foam in orange, yellow, and black; feathers
¼-inch moveable eyes
Thick white crafts glue
Pencil with round-tip eraser
Colored or patterned paper

HERE'S HOW

Puncture a small hole on each end of the egg. Break the yolk with a toothpick. Blow the inside of egg out into a bowl. Clean and dry egg.

For the fish
1. Draw a line around the egg, slightly above the middle. Paint the large area blue. Let it dry. Paint the remaining portion yellow. Paint a band of red in between.
2. Trace the fin and lips patterns, *page 77*, onto tracing paper and cut out. Trace the fin patterns onto yellow foam and the lips onto black. Cut out shapes and glue on the egg as shown, *below*. Position the side fins so that they support the fish upright. Glue on the eyes.
3. Paint white stripes on the blue. Add dots to the face by dipping the handle end of the paintbrush into black paint and dabbing on the egg.

For the yellow bird
1. Draw a line dividing the egg in half. Paint the top pink and the bottom yellow. Paint a band of black in between.

2. Dip a pencil eraser in black paint and dab on egg where eyes will be. Let dry. Glue eyes atop dots.
3. Trace beak and feet patterns, *page 77*, onto tracing paper and cut out. Trace beak pattern onto orange foam and feet onto black. Cut out and glue to egg as shown, *above*. Glue a feather in the top hole.

(continued on pages 76–77)

For the penguin

▼ **1.** Trace the patterns for the penguin, *opposite*, onto tracing paper and cut out. Place the heart-shaped face on the upper half of the egg and the teardrop shape on the bottom. Trace the shapes. Paint around the shapes using black. Let the paint dry.

2. Use the pattern to cut the bow tie from desired paper. Glue it near the bottom of the white heart shape.

▲ **3.** Glue the eyes on, positioning them inside the upper portion of the heart.

◄ **4.** Use the beak and feet patterns to cut shapes from orange foam. Fold the beak triangle in half lengthwise, holding it with a small dot of glue. Let it dry. Glue beak below eyes. Glue on the feet. Glue a feather in the hole in the top of the egg.

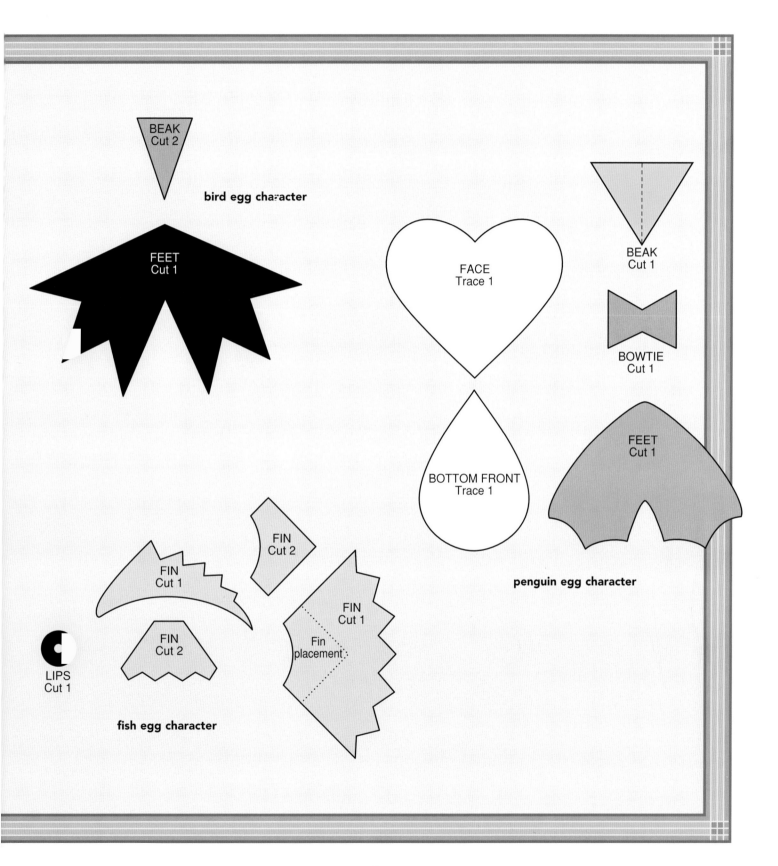

BEAK
Cut 2

bird egg character

FEET
Cut 1

FACE
Trace 1

BEAK
Cut 1

BOWTIE
Cut 1

BOTTOM FRONT
Trace 1

FEET
Cut 1

penguin egg character

FIN
Cut 2

FIN
Cut 1

FIN
Cut 1

Fin
placement

FIN
Cut 2

LIPS
Cut 1

fish egg character

oh-so-sweet watering can

With a splash of paint and a handful of decoupaged motifs, this watering can looks brand-new and ready for watering the garden or holding some of its bounty.

WHAT YOU'LL NEED
Metal watering can
Spray can of white primer paint
Acrylic paints in pink, white, red, and black
Foam plate
Sea sponge
½- and ⅛-inch flat paintbrushes
Greeting cards, wrapping paper, or envelopes to decoupage
Small scissors for fine cutting
Mod Podge decoupage medium
Thin wooden skewer
Clear varnish

(continued on pages 80–81)

HERE'S HOW

1. Begin with a clean dry surface. Spray the watering can with primer paint and let it dry.

◄ **2.** Place pink and white paints onto a foam plate. Soak the sponge with water before using and squeeze out excess water. Dip the sponge into the pink paint and dab onto the surface of the can. Then dip sponge into the white and dab on the can. Alternate sponging on the colors, dabbing the colors together. Keep a wet edge and continue sponging until the colors are blended as desired. Sponge the surface, overlapping into the areas to be painted red. Let the paint dry.

▲ **3.** Paint all the red areas using a larger brush for the larger areas. Use a small flat brush for the finer trim areas. It is okay to overlap into the white areas. Let the paint dry.
4. Paint the white areas next, cleaning up any overlapping red areas. This will probably take two or more coats. Let dry.

◄ **5.** Cut out desired motifs from greeting cards, wrapping paper, and envelopes using fine small scissors.

▲ **7.** Using a thin wooden skewer, dip into black paint and dot random dots onto the surface. Let the paint dry.

8. Coat the entire piece with two coats of clear varnish. Let the varnish dry.

▲ **6.** Brush a generous coat of decoupage medium on the back side of the cutout papers. Position each cutout where desired and paint over it again covering the front side with a coat of decoupage medium. Let dry.

a gathering of eggs

Snippets of ribbons...paper-punched shapes... quick paint strokes —you won't believe how easy it is to make these delicate, one-of-a-kind eggs. The instructions begin on page 85.

floral swirl egg

pretty primary egg

star-struck egg

dainty rose egg

carnation-topped egg

floral swirl egg

See photograph, page 82.

WHAT YOU'LL NEED
Egg
Toothpick
Acrylic paints in soft peach, coral,
 light moss green, and white
Paintbrush
Thick white crafts glue
White cording

HERE'S HOW
1. To blow out the egg, poke a
tiny hole on each end using a sharp
object. Pierce the egg yolk inside
with a toothpick. Blow out insides
into a bowl. Rinse and wipe dry.
2. Paint the egg soft peach. Let
the paint dry.
3. Run a thin line of glue around
the egg, coiling as you go (see
page 82). Carefully cover glue with
white cord. Let the glue dry.
4. Paint a row of tiny coral-colored
flowers between the rows of cord.
Dip the handle end of a paintbrush
in paint and dot onto the surface.
Let the paint dry. Use a toothpick
to make a white dot inside each
coral dot. To make leaves, add a
little green oval to the sides of
each flower.

pretty primary egg

See photograph, page 83.

WHAT YOU'LL NEED
Egg
Toothpick
Pencil with round-tip eraser
Acrylic paints in yellow, red,
 green, purple, blue, and light
 moss green
Paintbrush
Thick white crafts glue
Thin black rickrack

HERE'S HOW
1. To blow out the egg, poke a
tiny hole on each end using a sharp
object. Pierce the egg yolk inside
with a toothpick. Blow out insides
into a bowl. Rinse and wipe dry.
2. Draw pencil lines to divide the
egg into 8 sections, as shown on
page 83. Each side of the egg will
have four different colored
sections. Paint the sections red,
blue, light moss green, and purple.
Let the paint dry.
3. Make yellow flowers by dipping
the eraser end of a pencil into
yellow paint and dotting onto
surface. Let the paint dry. Dot a red
dot onto the center of each yellow
flower using the handle end of a
paintbrush. Paint green leaves next
to flowers. Let the paint dry.
4. Glue black rickrack onto egg
dividing colored sections.

star-struck egg

See photograph, page 83.

WHAT YOU'LL NEED
Egg
Toothpick
Acrylic paint in lavender and white
Paintbrush
Yellow paper
Star paper punches in two sizes
Thick white crafts glue

HERE'S HOW
1. To blow out the egg, poke a
tiny hole on each end using a
sharp object. Pierce the egg yolk
inside with a toothpick. Blow out
insides into a bowl. Rinse and
wipe dry.
2. Paint the egg lavender. Let the
paint dry.
3. Use the paper punches to cut
out various-sized yellow stars. Glue
the stars randomly onto the egg
(see *page 83*). Let the glue dry.
4. To add tiny dots, dip a
toothpick into white paint and dot
in a circle pattern around each star.
Let the paint dry.

ribbon and roses egg

dainty rose egg

See photograph, page 83.

WHAT YOU'LL NEED
Egg
Toothpick
Acrylic paints in light moss green
  and white
Paintbrush
Floral-patterned ribbons
Thick white crafts glue
Pink satin ribbon rose

HERE'S HOW
1. To blow out the egg, poke
a tiny hole on each end using a
sharp object. Pierce the egg
yolk inside with a toothpick.
Blow out insides into a bowl.
Rinse and wipe dry.
2. Paint one side of the egg solid
moss green. Place the unpainted
side down and rest egg in a small
glass to dry. Paint the other side.
Let dry.
3. Glue two bands of ribbon
around the egg, as shown on
page 83. Glue another ribbon
crosswise, dividing the egg
in half. Glue a satin ribbon rose
onto the center where ribbons
cross. Let the glue dry.
4. Add white dots by dipping
the handle end of a paintbrush
in white paint and gently dabbing
on the egg surface.

carnation-topped egg

See photograph, page 84.

WHAT YOU'LL NEED
Egg
Toothpick
Acrylic paints in black and white
Paintbrush
Red satin ribbon carnation
Thick white crafts glue

HERE'S HOW
1. To blow out the egg, poke
a tiny hole on each end using a
sharp object. Pierce the egg
yolk inside with a toothpick.
Blow out insides into a bowl.
Rinse and wipe dry.
2. Paint one side of the egg
black. Place the unpainted side
down and rest egg in a small
glass to dry. Paint the other side.
Let dry.
3. Add white dots by dipping
the handle end of a paintbrush
in white paint and gently dabbing
on the egg surface (see *page 84*).
4. Glue a red ribbon carnation
onto the top of the egg. Let the
glue dry.

ribbon and roses egg

See photograph, opposite.

WHAT YOU'LL NEED
Egg
Toothpick
Acrylic paints in pale yellow and
  light moss green
Paintbrush
Thick white crafts glue
Thin green ribbon
Red seed beads

HERE'S HOW
1. To blow out the egg, poke
a tiny hole on each end using a
sharp object. Pierce the egg
yolk inside with a toothpick.
Blow out insides into a bowl.
Rinse and wipe dry.
2. Paint one side of the egg solid
pale yellow. Place the unpainted
side down and rest egg in a small
glass to dry. Paint the other side.
Let dry.
3. Run thin lines of glue
around the egg, crossing both
ways as shown, *opposite.* Apply
the thin green ribbon onto the
egg. Let the glue dry.
4. Glue red beads in the center
of each yellow section. Let the
glue dry.
5. Paint two tiny green ovals by
each bead for leaves.

springtime topiary

Even the Easter Bunny will stop in his tracks to get a glimpse of this whimsical topiary made of painted wood.

WHAT YOU'LL NEED

One 1½-inch round wooden ball
Measuring tape and pencil
Drill with ¼- and ⅛-inch drill bits
Five 2½-inch wooden eggs
3½-inch terra-cotta flower pot
Acrylic paints in medium green,
   white, yellow, royal blue, sky blue,
   bright pink, pale pink, and
   light orange; paintbrush
Pencil with round-tip eraser
Scissors
Five 1-inch-long pieces of ⅛-inch
   dowel; ¾-inch-wide wooden
   tongue depressor
11-inch-long piece of ¼-inch dowel
Wood glue
Plaster of Paris
Shredded crinkled paper

HERE'S HOW

1. To mark the wooden ball for drilling, measure and mark the center of the ball every 1⅛ inch. Use a ⅛-inch bit to drill ½-inch-deep holes at markings. Use the ¼-inch bit to drill a large hole between two of the small holes. For the eggs, mark the center of each small end.

Use the ⅛-inch bit to drill holes where indicated, ½ inch deep.
2. Wash and dry the terra-cotta pot. Paint the base bright pink and the rim yellow. Let dry. Dip the pencil eraser into light orange and dab on the pink. Use the end of a small paintbrush to make royal blue dots on the yellow. Let dry.
3. For the leaf, use a scissor to cut one end of the tongue depressor into a point. Paint the depressor and the large dowel stem medium green. Let dry. Add large white dots to the leaf and small white dots to the stem. Let dry.
4. Paint the wooden ball yellow. Let dry. Add large light orange dots to the ball. Let dry.
5. Using the photographs, *opposite and above*, paint the eggs as desired. Let dry.
6. Put a small amount of wood glue in each drilled hole in ball. Press a small dowel into each hole. Push the ¼-inch dowel into larger hole. Wipe away any excess glue.
7. Put a small amount of glue in each egg hole and push the

painted eggs onto the dowels. Let the glue dry.
8. Mix a small amount of plaster of Paris according to the directions. Leaving approximately 1 inch at the top of the pot, pour the plaster in the pot (if needed, put a cardboard circle in the bottom to avoid leakage out the bottom drain hole). Place the dowel in the center of the pot and push to the bottom. Add the leaf to one side. Let the plaster set until firm and dry.
9. Fill the top of the pot with shredded paper.

summer

It's the season when playing outdoors is a grand adventure for all ages—the most welcoming, "sunshiniest" season of all—SUMMER! Join us as we salute this warm-weather time with lovely painted vases, inviting tea linens, and fun-to-paint wooden bowls that will tickle friends with delight.

flower-laden tea linens

You can have a tea party on a moment's notice with these colorful accessories gracing your table.

WHAT YOU'LL NEED

Tracing paper and pencil
Scissors
1¼ yards of green dotted fabric
6x6-inch pieces of fabric for each
   of the flowers in bright pink, blue,
   orange, yellow, purple, and
   turquoise
4x4-inch piece of fabric for each
   flower center in orange, hot pink,
   bright yellow, and purple
⅛ yard each of two different
   greens for leaves
½ yard of yellow stripe fabric
½ yard of lining fabric for cozy
4 yards of 1½-inch black-and-white
   checked ribbon
2 yards of ⅝-inch black checked
   ribbon for each napkin
1 yard of piping cord
⅛ yard of red fabric
Matching rayon machine
   embroidery threads
Yellow embroidery floss for flower
   details, optional
Fleece
Thread for machine quilting
Fusible webbing paper

HERE'S HOW

FOR TEA COZY
(finished size 9¼x12 inches)

1. Enlarge and trace the tea cozy pattern, *page 94*, onto tracing paper. Use the pattern to cut two shapes from green dotted fabric.

2. Trace flower patterns, *page 95*, onto tracing paper. Use patterns to cut shapes from coordinating fabrics. Fuse flowers onto the tea cozy front according to the placement diagram, *page 94*. Machine appliqué edges using matching threads.

3. Cut a 12x¾-inch strip from red fabric. Stitch strip to bottom of appliquéd area using a ¼-inch seam allowance. Cut and add a 3-inch yellow striped strip below the red strip.

4. Line the cozy front with fleece and machine-quilt around the flowers. Cut out the cozy back using the same pattern as for front.

5. Cover piping with green dotted fabric cut on the bias and stitch around curved edge. Make a fabric loop and stitch to center top. Stitch front to back. Clip seam. Turn.

6. Cut two lining pieces using cozy pattern. Stitch rounded edge. Slip lining fabric into cozy. Baste around bottom edge. Bind bottom edge with 1½-inch checked ribbon.

(continued on page 94)

FOR NAPKIN

(finished size 16x16 inches)

1. Cut green dotted fabric into a 16-inch square.

2. Appliqué one flower of choice from place mat (see patterns on *pages 96–97*) in one corner.

3. Bind the edge with ⅝-inch checked ribbon.

FOR PLACE MAT

(finished size 13x18½ inches)

1. Trace patterns, *pages 96–97*, onto tracing paper, and cut out. Use patterns to cut shapes from desired fabrics.

2. Arrange and fuse the flower shapes together, as shown on *page 96*. Fuse the flowers to the background fabric. Machine satin-stitch the edges.

3. Cut a 13x18½-inch piece from the backing fabric and fleece. Trim the edge of appliquéd piece, allowing a ¼-inch seam.

4. Cut ¾-inch strips from red fabric. Using a ¼-inch seam allowance, stitch red border around the appliqué. Cut 1¼-inch strips from yellow striped fabric. Stitch to red border. Place the fleece between the front and back. Machine-quilt around the flowers.

5. Bind edges with 1½-inch wide ribbon. Add details to tulip using straight stitches and French knots, if desired.

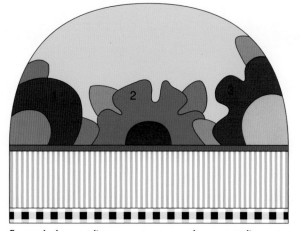

flower-laden tea linens — tea cozy placement diagram

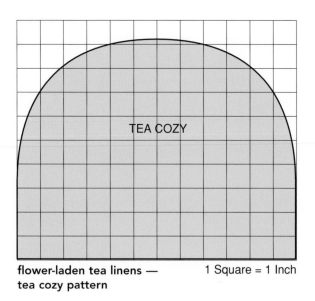

flower-laden tea linens — tea cozy pattern

1 Square = 1 Inch

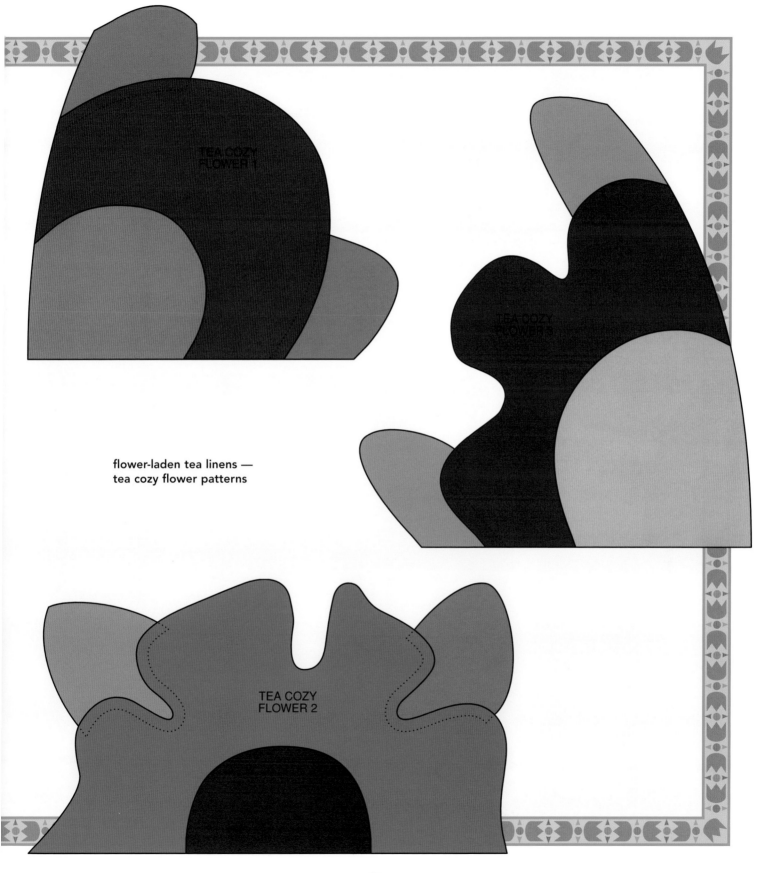

flower-laden tea linens —
tea cozy flower patterns

TEA COZY
FLOWER 1

TEA COZY
FLOWER 3

TEA COZY
FLOWER 2

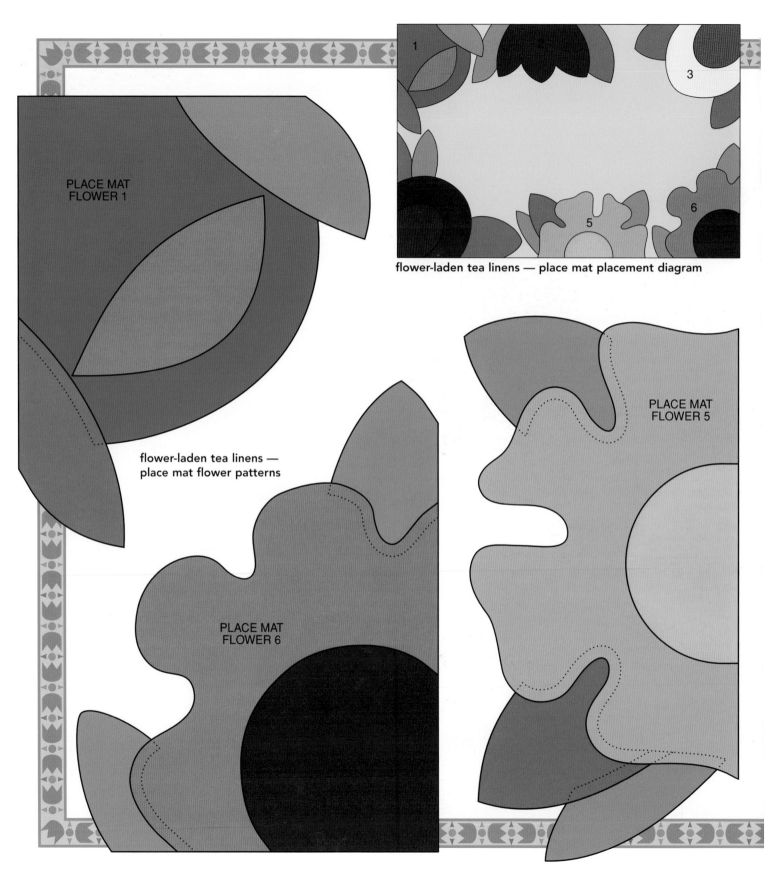

PLACE MAT
FLOWER 1

flower-laden tea linens — place mat placement diagram

flower-laden tea linens —
place mat flower patterns

PLACE MAT
FLOWER 5

PLACE MAT
FLOWER 6

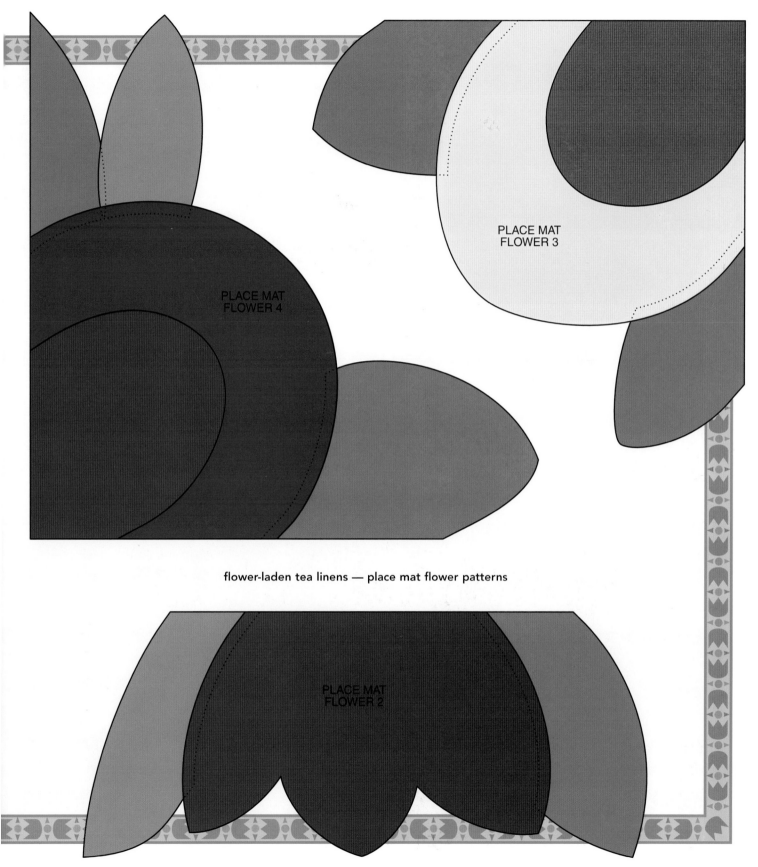

PLACE MAT
FLOWER 3

PLACE MAT
FLOWER 4

flower-laden tea linens — place mat flower patterns

PLACE MAT
FLOWER 2

a stack of "bowlies"

Once plain, these brightly painted bowls are ready to hold just about anything—or stack them in the center of the table for a very artful centerpiece.

WHAT YOU'LL NEED
Wooden bowls
Acrylic paints in red, blue, white, orange, yellow ochre, lime green, grass green, pink, and purple
Flat paintbrushes in various sizes
Pencil with round-tip eraser
Rubber band
Fine paintbrush
Clear varnish

HERE'S HOW
1. Paint large solid areas of bowls first. Paint the rim of the bowl after the inside and outside are painted, using a small flat brush.
2. To make dots around the outer edge of the bowl, dip the eraser end of a pencil in paint and dot onto the surface. When dry, add another colored dot over top of it, using the handle end of a paintbrush.
3. To make the vine design, place a large rubber band around the bowl where you want a continuous line. Mark with pencil and remove rubber band. Paint the line using a fine-pointed paintbrush. Paint the heart and the leaves.
4. When all paint is completely dry, finish with a clear coat of spray or paint-on varnish.

Note: We suggest using a glass or ceramic liner in any painted bowl when using with food.

sunny message tile

You'll love making and using this handy message tile—and so will your kids.

They may even want to make one for each of their favorite teachers!

WHAT YOU'LL NEED
Purchased wooden flower
Acrylic paints in yellow, green, brown, and red; paintbrush
Bakable clay; small stick
6-inch wooden ruler
Colored pencil
¼-inch-wide ribbon
6-inch square tile
Liquid Nails adhesive
Frame stand
Dry erase or water-based marker

HERE'S HOW
1. Paint the flower brown. Let dry. Paint the flower yellow, using very little paint on the brush. Paint from the outside working toward the center. Do not paint in the crevices, allowing the brown to show through. Paint the stem and leaves green. Let dry.
2. Roll a walnut-sized piece of clay into an apple shape. Flatten one side. Insert small stick into top to make a stem. Bake as directed by the manufacturer. Paint the apple red and the stem green. Let dry.
3. If the ruler is unpainted, paint it with a thin coat of yellow, allowing the markings to show. Let dry.
4. Glue all items on the tile using the photograph, *left*, as a guide.
5. Set tile in a frame stand. Use *only* a dry erase marker or water-based marker for writing.

glorious gourds

Adding color to the garden or dressing up an indoor planter, this birdhouse and its fluttering friends add a fun touch wherever they're perched.

WHAT YOU'LL NEED

Gourds: 2 small ornamental and
   one large gourd for birdhouse
Warm soapy water
Scrubber
Drill
1-inch drill bit and small bits
3 dowels: one ½-inch dowel and
   two ⅛-inch dowels cut to
   desired lengths
Acrylic paints in soft yellow, bright
   yellow, white, lime green, grass
   green, red, lavender, blue, black,
   and pastel blue
Pencil with round-tip eraser
Black permanent marker
2 wooden skewers
Thick white crafts glue
White crafting foam
Wire
Wire cutters
4 beads

(continued on pages 104–105)

HERE'S HOW

▼ Purchase gourds and allow to dry and "cure." If the gourds are green when you acquire them, they need to go through a curing stage. A gourd may mold, but it should be useable as long as it does not turn soft. It is ready to use when the surface is hard, dry, lightweight, brown, and feels hollow. Clean the gourd with warm soapy water and a scrubber. Scrape off any mold, rough areas, and the outer layer of dried skin. The surface should feel like smooth clean wood.

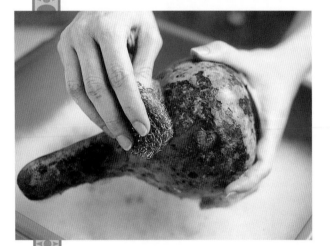

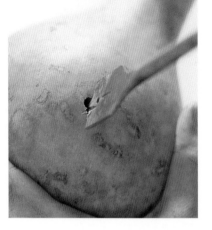

▲ **1.** To make the birdhouse shown on *pages 102–103*, first mark a spot for the hole. Drill a 1-inch hole into the gourd. Drill a ½-inch hole in the bottom to insert a ½-inch dowel.

2. Paint the bottom portion a soft pale yellow. Paint the top portion grass green. Paint a zigzag edge as shown on *page 103*. Add flowers in the green area. Make flowers by dotting paint onto the surface, with the eraser end of a pencil. Paint small half-circles for leaves, using lime green. Add smaller dots in the center of flowers using the handle end of paintbrush.

3. Paint a ring of bright yellow around the hole. Add red checks with a small flat brush.

4. Paint the dowel white and let dry. Add lime green stripes. Let it dry. Add glue to the end and insert into the bottom of the gourd.

Insects

1. Beginning with clean gourds, paint each a solid color, one soft yellow and one pastel blue. Let dry.

▼ **2.** For the bee, add black stripes using a permanent black marker, making vertical lines in a band around gourd. Add black dots for eyes.

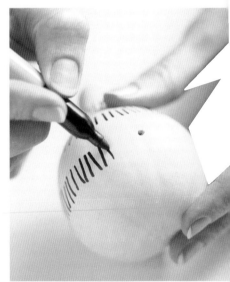

▲ **3.** Using photo *above* as a guide, drill five tiny holes in gourds, two for the antennae, two for the wings, and one for the stinger. Cut off the pointed ends of a wooden skewer and insert it through one side and out the other for the wings. Cut a 3-inch piece from the end of the remaining skewer. Paint it black and let dry. Glue the painted skewer piece into the hole in the small end of the gourd.

▶ **4.** Cut two small and two large ovals from white foam for wings. Glue onto the wooden skewer as shown *right*. Paint small wooden beads white and let dry. Attach the beads to the ends of the wire. Insert wire into gourd. Secure in place with glue if needed.

5. Paint ⅛-inch dowels white and drill another hole into the bottom of the insects. Insert the dowel, adding glue for extra support.

summertime florals

Goblets and vases of all shapes and sizes come alive with a few simple strokes of glass paint. Instructions begin on page 109.

**checkerboard band vase
and fluttering butterfly vase**

brilliant base goblet

checkerboard band vase

See photograph, page 106.

WHAT YOU'LL NEED

Clear glass vase
Glass paints in black, white, bright pink, and yellow; ½-inch flat brush
Pencil with round-tip eraser

HERE'S HOW

▼ **1.** Paint a white band around the center of the vase, approximately 1½ inches (this vase had a ribbed area, which we painted). Let the paint dry thoroughly.

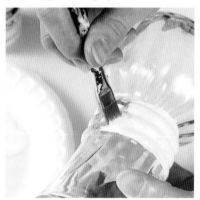

▶ **2.** Using a ½-inch flat brush, paint black checks every ½ inch as shown. Let the paint dry.
3. To add dots, dip a round-tipped pencil eraser into paint and dab carefully on the vase surface. Add pink dots to the base of the vase and yellow dots to the top portion. Let the paint dry.

fluttering butterfly vase

See photograph, page 106.

WHAT YOU'LL NEED

Clear glass vase
Glass paints in black, yellow, bright green, bright pink, and orange
Liner paintbrush
Small round paintbrush

HERE'S HOW

1. To make butterfly wings, use pink, orange, or green. Paint two dime- or nickel-size dots side by side for each butterfly, or paint four larger ovals in an "X" formation as shown. While the paint is wet, paint over the centers of the wings with yellow, blending the colors. Let dry.
2. Paint bodies, antennae lines, and wing detail using a liner paintbrush and black paint. Let dry.
3. To make dots on antennae and to show movement of butterflies, dip the handle end of a small paintbrush into black paint and dab on vase surface where dots are desired. Let dry.

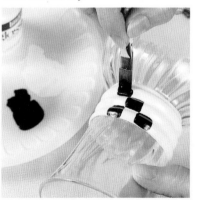

anything-but-blue vase

See photograph, page 107.

WHAT YOU'LL NEED

Colored bottle
Glass paints in black, white, red, pink, yellow, and lime green
Small flat paintbrush
Pencil with round-tip eraser
Tracing paper
Scissors
Wooden skewer or toothpick

HERE'S HOW

1. Outline a rectangular-shaped box and paint in solid black area. Let dry thoroughly and paint a second coat if needed. Paint a black band toward the top of the bottle.
2. Draw a small heart on paper. Cut the heart out and trace the shape onto the black square. Paint the heart red. Let it dry. Paint a second coat if needed.
3. Add random flowers in yellow and pink. Dip the eraser end of a pencil into paint and dot onto the surface. When dry, use a paintbrush handle to add the center dot. Add oval-shaped lime green leaves.
4. In the remaining areas, add white dots, using a wooden skewer or toothpick. Dip in the white paint and dot onto the black surface. Let the paint dry.

sunshine goblet vase

See photograph, page 107.

WHAT YOU'LL NEED

Goblet or glass with etched
 leaf pattern (often found at
 flea markets)
Wooden skewer the width of a
 toothpick
Glass paints in black, soft
 yellow, lime green, hot pink,
 and orange
Fine-point paintbrush and flat
 paintbrush

HERE'S HOW

*Note: This vase is being
painted on the inside, so it
should never be used for food
or drink.*
1. Make tiny black dots on
the inside of the goblet by
dipping the flat end of a
wooden skewer in black paint
and dotting carefully onto the
inside of the goblet. Make
random dots, avoiding the
vine area. Let the paint dry.
2. Paint the inside with
several coats of yellow paint
until it is well covered,
allowing paint to dry between
coats. If the goblet has a base
pedestal, paint the bottom.

3. Using a very fine-pointed
brush, paint the etched vine
area green. Paint a simple
orange tulip design over vine,
approximately every inch, as
shown on *page 107*. Using
desired floral colors, paint
circles around some of the black
dots, adding three tiny green
leaves around each circle.
4. Paint the beaded and
banded areas of the stem
black. Let the paint dry.

bubble bottle vase

See photograph, page 107.

WHAT YOU'LL NEED

Glass paints in yellow, green,
 magenta, purple, blue,
 and white
Paintbrush
Clear bottle with a bubble-like
 shape

HERE'S HOW

1. Paint each section of the
bottle a different color. It may
require two or three coats for
different colors. Let dry.
2. To add white dots, dip
the handle end of a small
paintbrush into paint and dot
onto the bottle. Let dry.

*Note for all vases:
Bake finished vase in the
oven if instructed by the
paint manufacturer.*

brilliant base goblet

See photograph, page 108.

WHAT YOU'LL NEED

Clear glass goblet
Glass paints in black, pink,
 red, periwinkle, yellow,
 green, and white; liner and
 small round paintbrushes
Pencil with round-tip eraser

HERE'S HOW

1. Paint the top of the base
black. Let the paint dry.
2. To make flowers, use pink,
red, or periwinkle. Paint
dime- to quarter-size dots on
base, leaving room between
flowers to add dots and
leaves. Let the paint dry.
3. Paint green oval leaves in
various sizes along sides of
the flowers. Use a round-tip
pencil eraser or the handle
end of a small paintbrush to
add flower centers in yellow.
Fill in base with small white
dots, made with the handle
end of a paintbrush. Let the
paint dry.
4. To add large dots, dip a
round-tipped pencil eraser
into white paint and dab
carefully on the vase surface.
Let the paint dry.

index

If you enjoy this book, look for these other craft titles from Mary Engelbreit.

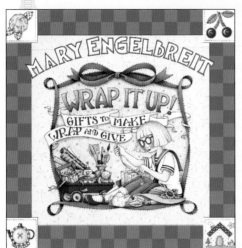

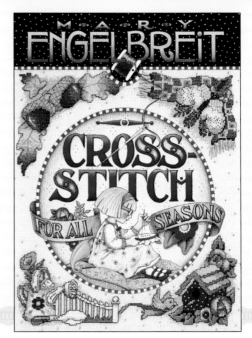